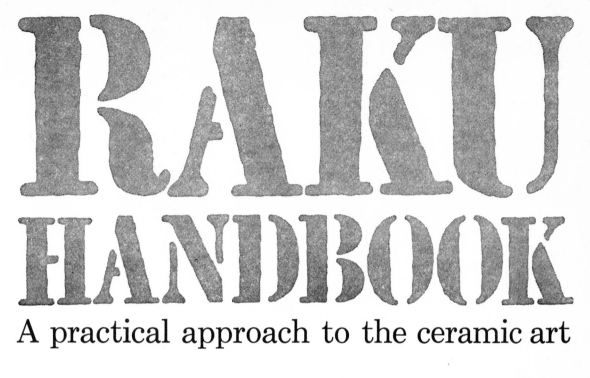

RAKU HANDBOOK

A practical approach to the ceramic art

John Dickerson

Van Nostrand Reinhold

Studio Vista London

Though you wipe your hands
And brush off the dust and dirt
From the Tea vessels
What's the use of all this fuss
If the heart is still impure?

Sen-no-Rikyu

Sign of Raku Tannyu
(1795-1854)

Copyright © 1972 by John Dickerson

First published in Great Britain 1972 and reprinted 1974 by Studio Vista
35 Red Lion Square, London WC1R 4SG
and in the United States of America by
Van Nostrand Reinhold Company
A Division of Litton Educational Publishing, Inc.
450 West 33rd Street, New York, N.Y. 10001
Van Nostrand Reinhold Company Regional Offices:
New York Cincinnati Chicago Millbrae Dallas
Van Nostrand Reinhold Company International Offices:
London Toronto Melbourne

Set in Monotype Times Roman
Printed in Great Britain by
Fletcher & Son Ltd, Norwich
Library of Congress Catalog Card Number 72–1442
ISBN (U.S.A.) 0 442 22092 8

ISBN (U.K.) 0 289 70241 0

Contents

1 Raku for everyone

Raku for everyone does not imply that this book seeks to reduce Raku to its lowest common denominator; indeed it does not, for such an approach would inevitably disregard those wide areas of the art in which the most subtle potentialities lie. Rather the aim is to show that the process of self-development through Raku can be available to all who seek it earnestly, whether they be established potters or students or indeed have neither training in ceramics nor access to the usual pottery equipment.

Raku forms

In Japan Raku has been mainly restricted to the traditional forms of those articles used in the Tea Ceremony and consisting primarily of Tea bowls, incense boxes and dishes. Within the general limitations of these forms the Raku potters have achieved a wide and brilliant range of variations. Classical Raku may be divided into two categories, denoted by the colours of the wares most commonly produced by each technique. They are *kuro* (black) and *aka* (red) Raku. These two types have differing firing techniques and each makes use of different clays and glazes. The type of Raku that is becoming popular outside Japan, and with which this book is concerned, combines the clay type and firing technique of black Raku with the glazing chemistry of red Raku.

The Tea Ceremony is peculiar to the Japanese culture; it would consequently be both pedantic and quite against the spirit of Zen to attempt merely to copy Japanese originals. And indeed, however fascinating we may find these master-pieces, the experience of personal exploration within the limitations of the technique is likely to be even more rewarding and exciting on a personal level. On the other hand, only a study of the traditional wares can reveal the unique aesthetic qualities that have been developed and that are possible through the Raku process.

Raku pieces are, for purely practical reasons, normally relatively small in size but there are very few other restrictions of form. Raku has a built-in process of natural selection that rejects many of those pieces that are poorly made, ill-considered and out of sympathy with the Raku spirit. But, provided that we work within these very broad limitations, we have a free rein to explore the whole spectrum of forms from the most carefully designed through to the most freely and accidentally produced that invention and interaction with the materials can achieve.

Materials

The raw materials for the production of Raku are cheap and easily available to all. They are the familiar elements of the potter's art and those that have traditionally been seen as constituting the primal elements of the universe: earth, air, fire and water. In Raku these elements have to be examined and their potentialities and limitations explored in depth until the potter arrives at a state of intuitive rapport with them. The fifth and most vital element is the maker and his attitudes, for ultimately it is his ideas, responses and personality that will condition the physical forms to be generated. It is the quality of these ideas and the degree of sensitivity and insight into the moving forces of nature that will determine the significance of the work.

Like all pottery, Raku is a ceramic ware made from clay, a substance which constitutes some two-thirds of the earth's crust. A clay with the special qualities required for Raku can be achieved simply by mixing selected locally occurring materials. A preliminary survey of the local geography will usually provide evidence of clay seams which can be dug, prepared, mixed and modified with additions of sand and other earth minerals to give the potter a personal and satisfactory material for making Raku.

Clays can, of course, be bought. Usually they come ready sieved and prepared, which eliminates most of the work involved in claiming clay direct from nature, and it is to be expected that most potters undertaking the making of Raku will generally make use of industrially prepared clays.

However, it should be stressed at this stage that the knowledge and experience gained by obtaining clay directly from nature should be attempted on at least some occasions, for besides providing the potter with his own 'personal' clay it will teach him more about the nature, structure and character of clay than can this or any book on the theory of clays. In addition to this, the digging of clay is a highly satisfying achievement, conducive to the establishment of that deep and extended intimate relationship between man and nature which is the basis of Raku.

Tools and their uses

One can justifiably advance the proposition that anything which can be manipulated can be used as a tool in making Raku – certainly, the idea that the Rakuist needs to buy a set of prescribed tools does not apply. Regular tools are, of course, useful but to rely upon them exclusively does seem to impose unnecessary and arbitrary limits. Anything and everything will somehow mark, cut, score, texture, pierce, shape or make an impression in clay. Tools are but extensions of the hands which are themselves extensions of the inquistive mind.

Since no two people work in exactly the same manner or even have physical conformity it is clear that mass-produced tools can be little more than a lowest common denominator of their requirements. The best tools are certainly those the potter makes to suit his personal requirements. These will fit more comfortably into the hand and will perform in accordance with the characteristics which the potter has built into them; and there is a much greater sense of identification and affinity with self-made tools which enables us, as far as is conceivably possible, to overcome the handicap of having to use a tool at all.

Similarly, the studio environment, with its machinery, furniture and routine patterns of behaviour as well as established methods of working clay, seems to have a detrimental and inhibiting effect on Raku, making it far more predictable and akin to other sorts of pottery. Raku pieces are best formed out in the open near where clay has been dug and prepared, worked with improvised tools, glazed with brushes made from dried grass and fired in the simplest of kilns. This kind of self-discipline and reliance on the ability to create pottery directly from nature is an important aspect of Raku. It is, furthermore, an interesting way of approaching the Zen dictum that a work of art must conform to the laws which govern nature.

Fig. 1
Full set of requirements for
Raku firing:
A Bisque kiln
B Fire clay box for carbon
shadow decoration
C Ample supply of fuel
D Kiln for glaze firing
E Containers of combustible
materials for secondary
reduction process
F Saggars for bisque and
glaze kilns
G Water for quenching wares
after removal from
secondary reduction
chamber
H Protective goggles and
asbestos gloves
I Chemicals for splashing on
molten glaze
J Saggar-lid hook
K Raku tongs
L Tamper
M Ash rake
N Wares made from suitable
clay body
O Vacuum cleaner (set to
reverse) or an air pump
(optional)
P Paraffin flame gun for
assisting in lighting kilns
(optional)

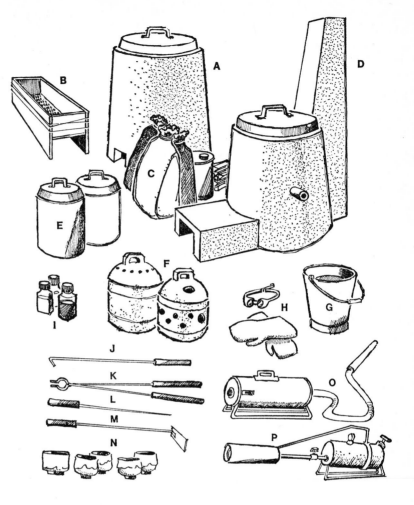

Technique

The Raku process is similar in theory to that used to produce the majority of potteries. Once the clay has been formed and allowed to dry, it is given a low first (or bisque) firing in a kiln. This firing serves to release chemically combined water from the clay, which is thereby converted into an irreversibly hard and stable material. This done, the pot is glazed. Glaze is made of silica and other materials suspended in an aqueous solution which form a surface coating on the pot as the liquid dries. When completely dry the pot is then fired for a second time – this causes the glaze chemicals to melt together to become a thin layer of liquid glass. As the pot cools the liquid glass hardens leaving the pot coloured, glossy and, to a large degree, non-porous.

But if Raku is similar to other types of pottery in basic theory it is radically different in technique and approach. The most obvious differences between Raku and other ceramic techniques lie in the methods of glaze firing and the continuous involvement of the potter throughout the whole process of production. In most ceramic processes other than Raku, pots for glaze firing are placed cold into a cold kiln chamber, after which the kiln is heated gradually until the required maturation temperature for the glaze is reached. The heating process normally takes many hours. When the glaze has finally melted the supply of heat to the kiln is discontinued and the pot is allowed to cool slowly within the kiln again over a period of many hours. It is not unusual for the whole firing cycle to take several days. When the pot is eventually removed from the kiln its surface, colour and texture are radically changed and, indeed, in many cases the piece is almost unrecognizable. The potter has lost contact with his issue during the critical stage of its development. His continuity of influence has been severed and the sensitive interaction between the two broken. What was once totally his own is now partly alien.

Raku firing bravely rejects the caution and impersonality of such a technique and boldly accepts the direct ordeal of sudden fire as an ultimate test of both pot and maker. The pot is plunged directly into a red-hot kiln by means of a pair of tongs and the kiln rapidly closed. If the pot survives the sudden heat shock its soft glaze melts within a few minutes under the constant surveillance of the potter who watches through a peep-hole in the side of the kiln. At the exact moment that he gauges the glaze to have matured and run in accordance with his wishes the kiln is quickly opened and the fiery pot, coated with glowing molten glaze, is snatched from the fire. At this point the pot is sometimes thrown into combustible materials, which ignite causing random patterns of reduction and surface texture which can at any stage be 'frozen' into the pot by quenching it in cold water. On other occasions the red-hot pot is taken from the kiln and thrust directly into water.

The ordeal and the experience are two-fold for, since the pot is in every way an extension of the maker, he too in a very real way is subjected to test by ordeal. The quality of the pot reflects the quality of the man, and the outcome of its trial, be it triumphant beautification or a piece irrevocably scarred or apparently soberly detached, necessarily carries over its experience to its maker. Since each piece and each firing are unique events the results are always startlingly different and unrepeatable, but the value goes far beyond the pot alone, for it represents a chronicled history of one man's direct struggle with the unpredictable forces of nature and a dual involvement in the dramatic 'process of becoming'.

2 Historical background

The Ashikaga period of Japanese history (1338–1573) was marked by an insidious escalation of internal military conflicts between the numerous local feudal lords across the country as they struggled to enlarge both their territories and their influence. This situation, which wrought havoc at all levels of Japanese life, had evolved over a period of several centuries. The Emperor had initially been manoeuvred out of real control of the country in the ninth century by the courtly family of Fujiwara. The Emperor continued, however, as nominal head-of-state (as well as remaining as head of the Shinto religion), but henceforth he lacked the power to enforce political demands.

The Fujiwara family themselves eventually slipped from power. Their essentially courtly nature and almost exclusive concern with affairs of the court and capital were instrumental in their downfall, for it divorced them from the feudal society that was developing in provincial Japan. In due course it was the most powerful feudal factions that replaced the court control with a series of military governments, each under the leadership of its general in chief (Shogun). These military governments (*bakafu*) perpetuated the Fujiwara tradition of allowing the Emperor to retain his nominal position, while the real power moved into the hands of the Shogun and his military leaders.

During the fourteenth century the Ashikaga clan superseded the former military régime of the Hojo at Kamakura and established a new Shogunate at Kyoto. Although this government was maintained until 1568 it was weak and its ability to control the nation became progressively more ineffectual. As a result the country sank into a long period of bitter feudal conflict.

The Kamakura and Ashikaga periods did, however, produce some significant changes in Japanese life which were to affect profoundly its future social and cultural development. Most notably they brought about the establishment of a new political and social élite in the form of the professional warrior (*Samurai*) class. Not only the sword but also the philosophical attitudes, codes of behaviour and aesthetic taste of the *Samurai* became prominent features of Japanese life.

It was at this time that Zen Buddhism rose to a position of dominating philosophical importance. The Zen religion had been given its first firm roots in Japan during the twelfth century by the monks Eisai and Dogen who had returned from periods of studying the Ch'an Buddhist religion in Southern-Sung China. ('Zen' is a Japanese transliteration of the Chinese word 'Ch'an'.) Like the other Buddhist sects that emerged in medieval Japan, Zen aimed at bringing salvation within the grasp of the common man, but while the other sects proposed a route through faith in external agencies Zen offered salvation through personal effort.

The basis of Zen lies in the belief that Buddha-nature exists as a real potential within every man and that it can be attained through looking into one's true inner nature with self-understanding. Its tools are meditation and intensive self-reliance (and, in Rinzai Zen, a deliberate 'shock' treatment designed to overcome the limitations of rational or logical thought processes). It is through these practices and a deep involvement in life's activities that the key to man's place in the macrocosm may be found. Thus Zen sees that the path to salvation lies in commitment to the 'process of becoming' rather than to end products (which by definition have lost the dynamic for further 'development'), and proposes that even the simplest and most mundane activities and objects have great beauty and great significance because they can be the vehicles by which enlightenment is attained. 'Reality' and the 'moment of truth' lie in the immediacy of actual experience in present time; this belief, together with Zen's emphasis on intuitive response, austerity, advancement through personal devotion, action and stern masculinity all contributed to make it the ideal philosophy for the *Samurai* class.

Through the *Samurai* class Zen exerted a massive influence on Japanese life and art which was to leave an indelible print on the national personality. It was particularly fostered under the Ashikaga Shoguns, Yoshimitsu and Yoshimassa, both of whom were ardent supporters of the sect and men of refined and aesthetic temperaments. Among their favourite Zennist activities was the drinking of powdered tea in the company of artistic friends, while practising such arts as painting and composing poems. These gatherings, known as *Cha-e*, were the beginning of the Tea Ceremony cult which, more than any other art form, was to mould Japanese aesthetic life.

The decade 1560–70 witnessed the emergence of three great men of political and military genius, who were to pacify and revitalize the nation. They were Oda Nobunaga (initially a comparatively minor feudal lord), Toyotomi Hideyoshi (an adventurer of low birth and spectacular abilities who attached himself to Nobunaga, became his lieutenant and eventually succeeded him as the supreme military force in Japan) and Tokugawa Ieyasu, a feudal lord and statesman who succeeded to the Shogunate after the eventual downfall of the House of Toyotomi.

Oda Nobunaga was responsible for initiating the movement that was, under Hideyoshi, finally to break the great cycle of wars that had plagued Japan for so long. Lord Oda was a man of astute mind, ruthless determination and military ability who had the extreme good fortune to have the services of Hideyoshi, undoubtedly one of the most brilliant tacticians and resourceful politicians the world has ever known. Nobunaga, largely through Hideyoshi's brilliant planning of his campaign, finally elevated himself to a position of military dominance in central Japan, from which he acted as protector of the established régime until he finally deposed the Ashikaga Shogun and ushered in a new era known as the Momoyama period (1568–1615).

The national policy that was followed by Nobunaga until his death in 1582 and thereafter by Hideyoshi was a two-fold one of moving towards a peaceful and unified nation by virtue of force of arms where negotiation failed, while at the same time directing the energies of the people towards positive and constructive ends. In pursuit of these goals Hideyoshi sapped the financial resources of the feudal lords (formerly used for military expenditure) and diverted this, and much of the manpower, to the building and repair of national monuments. He also encouraged new industries, showing particular personal interest in ceramics and, perhaps most significantly of all, threw the full weight of his support behind the Tea Master, Sen-no-Rikyu.

Under the patronage of Yoshimassa, the priest Shuko had begun a process of refining the *Cha-e* through emphasizing its Zennist qualities of dignity and severely restrained simplicity; the result was a formal but highly aesthetic ritual which welded all the Zennist arts into a sober yet rich experience.

Sen-no-Rikyu devoted great attention to individual aspects of the *Cha-e* and elevated each to a role of unprecedented artistry within what we might today describe as 'an environmental happening' that synthesized all its elements into a spiritually expanding yet mentally relaxing experience.

Rikyu's re-conceived Tea Ceremony (called *Cha-no-yu*) had extended its Zennist characteristics and particularly laid stress on the qualities of purity, peacefulness, austerity and abstraction. He received Hideyoshi's firm support in the democratic nature of *Cha-no-yu* for the practical purpose of bringing together traditional enemies in a spirit of amicability, for humbling the arrogant and generally exerting a calming influence on a nation grown tense and nervous with long years of war.

Rikyu's Tea Ceremony and his outstanding personal talents were both recognized and used by the shrewd Hideyoshi to establish *Cha-no-yu* in a position of unrivalled social and cultural importance, where it acted in many ways as the axis of both Hideyoshi's constructive policies and a new national aesthetic.

Among the elements of Rikyu's *Cha-no-yu* was a movement away from the old *Cha-e* 'taste' in ceramic wares. The vogue for the Chinese Temmoku bowls was replaced with a popularization of the Korean peasant Ido wares, whose unpretentious and unselfconscious appearance was more closely aligned with Rikyu's ideal of '*wabi*'.

Hideyoshi's policy of fostering the development of native industries was again echoed in Rikyu's philosophy of 'suitability for Tea', in which natural appearance takes precedence over the contrived, simplicity over the exotic and the local over the imported. These dogmas acted as a great spur to the Japanese ceramic industry and stimulated rich and numerous developments in many parts of the country.

In his search for a native ceramic ware that fully embodied all the spirit and attitudes of *wabi-cha*, Rikyu discovered the work of a Kyoto family of sculptor-potters headed by Chojiro. Chojiro was the son of a Korean immigré named Amaya (he had later taken the Japanese name of Sasaki Sokei). Both Amaya and his Japanese wife were potters. Amaya's speciality had been the production of the sculpted ceramic roof tiles that were used on all the most important buildings of the time, but, besides these, both he and his wife produced bowls for the Tea Ceremony. The family had, between them, invented a new process for the making of Tea bowls that involved a totally hand-made forming method followed by a rapid firing and cooling process, which essentially involved the artist in an intimate and sensitive rapport with his wares throughout their whole production. The results bore witness to the immediacy of the technique and captured the essence of the natural process.

Rikyu probably made his first contact with Chojiro after the death of Amaya, when Chojiro was operating the kiln with the help of an assistant and his sons. The distinctive sobriety of the work from the Chojiro kiln must have greatly impressed the great Rikyu, for he entered into collaboration with Chojiro to design and produce the ultimate in Tea wares. The bowls which they evolved over the years of collaboration and from subsequent commissions rank among the finest of Japan's ceramic wares and established a major precedent for the Tea wares of future generations.

Certainly the combination was a most fortunate one; an eminently suitable technique, an aesthetician possibly unsurpassed in human history and a family of sculptors with the ability to create forms that synthesized Rikyu's many specific requirements, yet retained their artistic unity and vitality.

Rikyu himself was so pleased with Chojiro's work on his behalf that he invested the sculptor with his own name and from this time on the maker of Rikyu wares was known as Tanaka Chojiro. In addition to the patronage of that great *Chajin*, Chojiro also gained the support of Rikyu's grandson Sotan (himself to become the greatest *Chajin* of his day), many *daimyos* (feudal barons – literally 'great names') and, not least, the supreme warlord, Hideyoshi, himself.

After the death of Chojiro, Jokei, the ablest of the sons, managed the kiln, enjoyed the same patronages and developed the styles of the first generation. Jokei extended the range of forms and developed a *shiro* (white) glaze to add to *aka* and *kuro* (red and black).

In recognition of Chojiro's achievement, Hideyoshi presented Jokei with the title 'Best in the World' and a golden stamp bearing the character RAKU (meaning ease, pleasure, enjoyment) and authorized it to be impressed on the wares from his kiln. Since that time many of the wares of Jokei and his family descendants have been stamped with the character and the family has taken the name 'Raku'. Hideyoshi's original stamp was lost by Jokei and succeeding generations have used one or more designs of the character as marks of identification (plate 4).

The influence of Rikyu eventually became so extensive in Japan that Hideyoshi (who was in any case a capricious and dangerous man to have as a patron – while Rikyu was high-principled and outspoken) considered him a personal threat to his authority and (after what must have caused him grave mental conflict, for the *Chajin*'s contribution to Hideyoshi's cause had been very great) took advantage of some minor incidents to order Rikyu to commit *seppuku* (*hara-kiri*).

This disaster could well have meant the demise of both the Sen and Raku families. As it transpired, however, this was not the case. Rikyu's son Shoan was granted his father's house and, although they retired from the political stage, the family continued to command great influence in the highest ranks of Tea.

Rikyu's grandson Sotan (Ganpaku) was a worthy descendant of his famous grandfather. He continued as the primary patron of Raku, and won back all

Masters of the Raku tradition

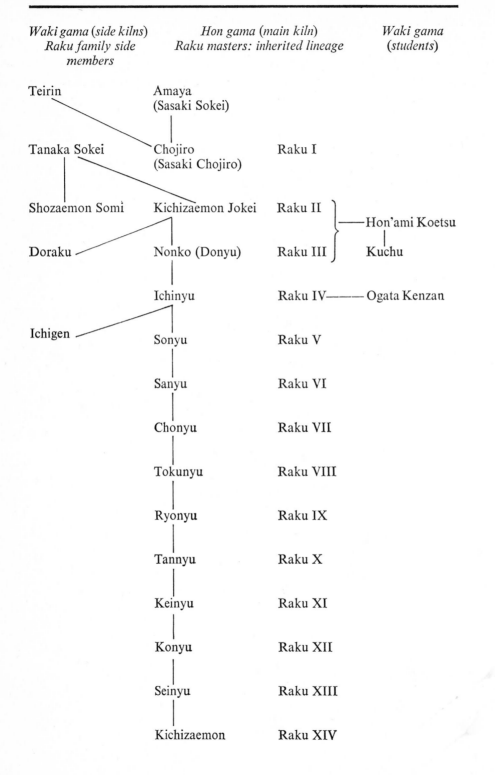

Waki gama (side kilns) Raku family side members	Hon gama (main kiln) Raku masters: inherited lineage		Waki gama (students)
Teirin	Amaya (Sasaki Sokei)		
Tanaka Sokei	Chojiro (Sasaki Chojiro)	Raku I	
Shozaemon Somi	Kichizaemon Jokei	Raku II	Hon'ami Koetsu
Doraku	Nonko (Donyu)	Raku III	Kuchu
	Ichinyu	Raku IV	Ogata Kenzan
Ichigen	Sonyu	Raku V	
	Sanyu	Raku VI	
	Chonyu	Raku VII	
	Tokunyu	Raku VIII	
	Ryonyu	Raku IX	
	Tannyu	Raku X	
	Keinyu	Raku XI	
	Konyu	Raku XII	
	Seinyu	Raku XIII	
	Kichizaemon	Raku XIV	

Rikyu's former possessions. After the death of Hideyoshi and the establishment of the strong Tokugawa Shogunate (1615–1867) Sotan served as a Tea Master to the Shogunate. As such he was immensely fortunate to have the services of one of the greatest individual sculptor-potters in Japanese history, Nonko, the third generation of Raku.

Nonko (also known as Donyu) demonstrated considerable creativity within the confines of the requirements of *Cha-no-yu* wares and substantially extended the range of forms, moods, decorative devices and glazes in the Raku vocabulary. He experimented with a wide variety of glaze compositions and improved kiln designs, which resulted in the now famous Raku glaze styles of *maku gusuri*, *nagare*, etc.

Of all the Raku masters Nonko's work is possibly the most deserving of careful study for, besides exhibiting a supreme response to the plastic qualities of his materials, his œuvre as a whole constitutes one of the most penetrating investigations into the crucial relationship that exists between concept, form, touch and appearance in the art of ceramics.

The Raku family, now in its fourteenth generation from Chojiro, still continues to work at its traditional art in Kyoto. During this time the quality of the Raku products has inevitably varied, but the temptation to classify them on the basis of merit must be avoided initially if one is to recognize the achievement of the Raku as a whole. At all generations we find a high level of creative awareness and a sensitive response to materials which has flowed out of synthesized involvements in the drama of process, precedent and the intellectual/physical problems-in-depth posed by the art. These have been additionally stimulated by the fact that each Master has deliberately re-conceived the art for himself and has thereby prevented it from lapsing into a mere inbred regurgitation of past formulas.

From the hands of this family has come down one of the finest, most sensitive and extended explorations of the possible variations within a very definite theme that any of the arts has ever produced. Contained at various points within it are solutions ranging from perception to genius.

Few countries outside Japan have produced an art resulting from this kind of extended personal involvement. We too can experience similar insights through involvement in the process.

3 Clay for Raku

Raku, in common with all other types of pottery, is made from clay. Of all the basic materials used by artists in the production of their artefacts clay is probably the most easily obtained, the cheapest and one of the most durable; yet it is unrivalled in the range of its potentialities for exploring form and plastic expression.

All pottery forms are the result of an interaction between the artist and his clay. This cannot be a one-way process in which the artist exercises a rigid and totally authoritarian control, for the result of such domination is a cold and lifeless product. All good pots, and good Raku pots in particular, are born of a sympathetic dialogue between the concepts and manipulations of the artist on the one hand and the nature of the material on the other. These two entities have to reach an understanding – a state of compromise in which each gives freely to the other. This synthesis is the form.

Because precise circumstances are unrepeatable every pot is particular and unique. In Raku the additional discipline of deliberately incorporating chance-occurrence as just one equal member among the other elements used in the process serves to produce wares which are more idiosyncratic than those made by other processes. Pots are, therefore, very like people and Raku pots like highly individual people. In recognition of this fact, Japanese Tea Masters give Raku pots individual names and accord them the respect due to honoured members of the community.

Raku pots are formed from plastic clay, are modified during the drying process and then fired and glazed. The first stage in the production of a good Raku pot must therefore involve the potter with his primary material and his most fundamental sensibility, which is the awareness of the possibilities of clay as a medium.

The origin and nature of clay

Clay is one of the most common constituents of the earth's crust. It is an earth mineral, formed as a result of erosion and atmospheric weathering of the planet's outer layers, which were themselves the result of the cooling of the surface layers of igneous rocks and minerals in the earth's infancy. During the millennia that followed massive forces have modified that surface through natural mechanics and chemical reaction. Erosion by weathering, the splitting of rocks through expansion and contraction, the movement of glaciers together with the solubility of some of the earth's constituents in water and the decomposing effects of acids have all played their part in breaking down the igneous crust and mixing the resulting fractured rock fragments and minerals. The deposit of fine rock particles laid down by this process has been largely freed of soluble materials and is what we know as clay.

Clay is composed of minute flat particles, a fact of great significance, for when these flat particles are aligned within a slaked mass they impart to the material a remarkable strength and self-supporting quality.

The name given to pure clay is kaolinite and its chemical formula is written $Al_2O_3.2SiO_2.2H_2O$.

Clays can be grouped into two main categories: Primary (or residual) and secondary (or transported). Primary clays, the result of erosion and chemical action, remain on the site of their formation. These residual clays tend to be chemically pure and are composed of particles of irregular size.

Secondary clays are those which have been carried by wind or water from their place of formation and deposited elsewhere. As one might expect, they tend to have gathered more impurities and organic matter than residual clays, but further interaction with the elements has generally reduced their average particle size as well as making them more uniform. Besides containing minerals and other impurities from foreign bodies, secondary clays tend to be a composite of various types of clays that have been transported from a number of sources to be deposited together.

The physical qualities of clay

Plasticity
The most significant quality of clay is its plasticity, which allows it to be freely manipulated and formed into any given shape and to retain that shape as it dries. The plasticity of clay is probably due to four main factors:
1 The extreme minuteness of the size of the constituent particles, often measuring as little as 0·5 of a micron in diameter.

2 The smooth flat form of the individual particles.
3 The presence of colloidal fluids formed from organic impurities in the clay.
4 A degree of ionization and electro-chemical attraction between the particles.

When the clay mass is impregnated with water each particle becomes coated with a fine lubricating film which allows smooth fluid manipulation of forms with the material. In both the wet and dry states the overlap of the myriad flat particles assists in supporting the form and imparting a high degree of mechanical strength to the material.

Plasticity is an essential quality in any working clay and is possessed in varying degree by the differing clay types. Should you find your clay to be either too plastic (slick, sticky, difficult to work, high degree of shrinkage with cracking) or excessively non-plastic (clay crumbles, pots break apart during forming) it must be modified: in the latter case by adding plastic clay, or, as in the former instance, by mixing a percentage of non-plastic material such as sand or grog with the clay.

Reaction to fire
In its unfired state clay is held together by its mechanical structure and physically combined water. As clay dries the physically combined water evaporates. The dry form is fragile and must be handled with considerable care. Dry strength may generally be thought of as increasing in proportion to the amount of plastic materials in the clay body. Because of the relatively high levels of non-plastic constituents in Raku bodies the dry pots or forms tend to be very fragile.

Upon being fired to the point at which chemically combined water is released from the molecule (at about 700 °C) clay becomes a hard and irreversibly rock-like substance of extreme durability and once again bears many of the characteristics of its parent rock.

An appropriate degree of heat will cause any clay to vitrify and, beyond that, melt. Most clays contain impurities which affect the clay's reaction to heat. Substances which cause the maturation processes to take place at lower temperatures are called fluxes and those which retard the process are termed refractory.

Colour
The colour of a specific clay is normally a factor of minor significance except inasmuch as it gives the potter an indication of the type of impurity contained. This may affect its usefulness. Red clays, for example, are normally high in iron content. This powerful flux can be expected to render the clay suitable only for a low firing range. Black clays commonly result from the presence of coal particles which have to be removed by screening. Dark grey clays normally contain organic impurities which burn away during firing.

Clay types for Raku bodies

The physical and chemical requirements of clays suitable for the making of Raku are such that the majority of clays are by themselves unsuitable. Because of this a calculated combination of various clays is used in which each constituent provides one or more of the required characteristics. This combination is known as a 'clay body'.

The types of clays most commonly used as components in Raku bodies are outlined below.

Kaolin (kaolinite)
Kaolin, also known as china clay, is the usual name for the pure primary clay

(kaolinite). It is pure white in colour, usually non-plastic and, since it withstands high temperatures, has a refractory effect in Raku bodies. Kaolin cannot be used alone to make Raku, but it can be a valuable component mainly for the purpose of adding strength to the fired form. Kaolin may constitute 0–20 per cent of a Raku body. For some special bodies this amount may be increased to 30 per cent.

Ball clay

Ball clay is similar to kaolin in its chemical composition; however, its characteristic qualities as a body component are almost totally opposite. Ball clay normally contains considerable organic matter and, more significantly, impurities of iron which make it much more fusible than kaolin. Ball clay is of small and even particle size and is incorporated into a Raku body to increase plasticity and workability. It also greatly increases the strength of dry or near dry forms and for this reason is a valuable component of the coarser bodies intended for carving. Ball clay may constitute up to 30 per cent of a Raku body.

Stoneware clay

Stoneware clays are plastic secondary clays, usually white, grey or buff in colour with a maturation temperature of around 1200 °C. Stoneware clays are the primary basic material for most types of studio pottery. Although unsuitable for Raku without the addition of other materials, stoneware clay does normally form the basis of Raku bodies produced by the 'compounding' and 'modification' methods. Limits: 0–60 per cent.

Fireclay

The term 'fireclay' does not so much apply to a specific clay type as to the implication of a very high degree of resistance to heat.

Fireclay may be obtained in either plastic or non-plastic forms; the more plastic varieties particularly make an excellent basis for Raku bodies. Almost all Raku bodies contain some fireclay, the usual content being within the range 10–50 per cent.

Saggar clay

Saggar clays have many properties in common with fireclays. Intended for the production of the boxes in which ceramic wares, including Raku, are placed to protect them from the direct effect of flames during the firing process, saggar clays are highly refractory and make either an excellent basis for Raku bodies or an important additive to increase thermal shock resistance. Saggar clays are often quite plastic in nature and form one of the few categories of clay that can be used for Raku pots with only the addition of grog.

Earthenware clays

Earthenware clays constitute the vast preponderance of all clays to be found in nature. They are usually red or brown in colour after firing due to the presence of considerable amounts of iron. Besides iron, earthenware clays commonly contain other fluxes, sand and mineral impurities. The presence of such large amounts of flux causes the clay to mature and tighten at low temperatures. This renders them useless by themselves for making Raku. However, dug earthenware clays can often be used after some modification with high firing materials. Industrially separated and prepared earthenware clays are normally used to impart colour to Raku bodies or to assist in increasing plasticity. Limits: 0–30 per cent.

Local brick clays

Deposits of brick clay can be found in many parts of Britain, Europe and the U.S.A. These are usually red-burning clays and contain large amounts of impurities such as coarse sand and fine gravel.

Brick clays are one of the few categories of clay which are, by themselves, usable for Raku wares and need only to have stones and large organic impurities removed before use. (Very many deposits of brick clay are free from impurities and may be used without any refinement.) Occasionally brick clays are unsuitable due to their lack of plasticity. This can, however, be simply remedied by the addition of a plasticizing clay.

Local brick clays provide one of the most attractive and inexpensive sources of Raku material. It is worth consulting a local library or geological office for details of occurrence in your area.

More advanced makers of Raku may be interested to experiment with additions of small percentages of the following materials. They should be strongly calcined before use.

Bauxite

A hydrated alumina often occurring in combination with clay and oxides of titanium and iron.

Spodumene

A lithium aluminum-silicate ($Li_2O.Al_2O_3.4SiO_2$) which after calcining to 950 °C exists in an irreversible β form. The low and even negative coefficients of expansion which we associate with the lithium aluminum-silicates such as spodumene recommend themselves to the Raku potter as an aid in ultra-fast firing and thermal shock resistance. Additions of spodumene β to Raku bodies can be expected to raise thermal stability by producing a lower average coefficient of expansion and also by absorbing free silica in the body into solid solutions (see quartz inversion below).

The familiar problems of glaze 'fit' resulting from lithium body components may prove as attractive to the Rakuist as they are undesirable to the industrial ceramist.

Petalite

Petalite ($Li_3.Al_2O_3.8SiO_2$) reacts in much the same way as spodumene in the Raku body and can also be used as an additive after calcination.

Other Raku body components

Quartz and flint

Quartz and flint are forms of silica and may be used as additions to Raku bodies to assist in increasing strength and the refractory nature of the body. The type known as macrocrystalline flint is the most desirable. Use less than 10 per cent to avoid dunting.

Note on quartz inversion: Quartz inverts from its a form to a β form at 573 °C with a sudden expansion of 2·2 per cent. Free quartz is converted to tridymite at 870 °C with an abrupt expansion of 15 per cent. Free quartz reverts back to its a form, with corresponding contractions, upon cooling. Such abrupt changes can cause severe strains on the body.

Sand
Sand is an impure silica usually combined with amounts of iron. It is used to open up Raku bodies for increased porosity and may substitute for all or part of the grog content.

Grog
Grog is the potter's term for clay which has been fired and then ground down into a granular form for use in clay bodies. Grogs are classified by their granular size. Commonly used sizes and classifications are:

100 mesh and smaller	very fine
100–80 mesh	fine
80–40 mesh	medium
40–20 mesh	coarse
Larger than 20 mesh	very coarse

The grades of grog selected for use in any particular Raku body will depend upon the method of pot forming to be employed. A body intended for thrown wares, for example, would not contain the coarser grades.

Grog normally constitutes a minimum of one-third of the bulk of Raku bodies; often the percentage is considerably higher. Sand or other refractory materials mentioned may substitute for a percentage of the grog.

Grog performs three important functions in the clay body:
1 opens up the body, making it more porous,
2 reduces expansion and contraction stresses,
3 increases tolerance to thermal shock.

Flint clays
Flint clays are non-plastic, refractory and primarily kaolinitic. Deposits also contain various amounts of diaspore or boehmite. Flint clays may be used to replace part of the grog content in Raku clay bodies.

Molochite
A refractory material similar to grog but produced from pre-fired china clay. It has a PCE > 1770 °C and, though expensive, is sometimes used as a substitute for grog when a particularly white body is required.

Volcanic ash
Volcanic ash is similar in chemical composition to granite. Small percentages may be added to help impart toughness to the body and reduce dunting.

Talc (steatite) $3MgO.4SiO_2.H_2O$
Small percentage additions of talc may be made to Raku bodies in order to improve the bonding of particles in the fired wares. Limits: 0–10 per cent.

Bentonite $Al_2O_3.4SiO_2.9H_2O$ + impurities
Bentonite is derived from volcanic ash and is characterized by its extreme minuteness of particle size. Bentonite is particularly useful in increasing the plasticity of a body, in which respect it is several times more effective per unit weight than ball clay. Limit: about 3 per cent, which, as a powder, should be thoroughly mixed into the dry body before it is slaked.

Feldspar
Small amounts of feldspar may be included in a Raku body to help promote body bond. Limits: 0–5 per cent.

The problems of thermal shock

The unique Raku technique subjects its wares to a series of sudden and severe rises and falls in temperature. Most types of ceramic ware would shatter under similar conditions, but Raku clay is specifically designed to withstand this kind of thermal shock.

In order to understand how a clay can be made proof against thermal shock and other firing process damage we must consider why it occurs in other wares.

The main causes are:
1 stresses set up within the walls of the pot by the expansion of trapped air during firing.
2 stresses set up within the form by chemically and physically combined water forcing an escape route.
3 stresses caused by the sudden expansion and contraction of chemicals changing form, e.g. quartz inversion.
4 inability of a ware to withstand non-uniform heat levels at various points, e.g. in thick and thin parts of the form or on the inner and outer surfaces.
5 incompatible coefficients of expansion and contraction of constituent particles with the body.

The causes of damage, therefore, fall into three categories:
1 & 2 The dense structure of the clay does not allow gases to escape freely. This can be alleviated by keeping the pores of the clay open. In Raku this is done by introducing considerable amounts of grog into the clay body.
3 A specific remedy can only be offered here in response to a specific problem, but the kind of corrective measures that would have to be employed are:
a introduce industrial chemicals such as spodumene β into the body to offset these stresses,
b introduce the chemical in a form where the change will not occur, e.g. in a calcined form,
c design the clay body so that the offending substance will not be present in a free form,
d substitute an alternative material,
e decrease the density and bond within the body.
4 & 5 These stresses most commonly occur at or near the point of vitrification or when the body is dense and closely bonded. Raku bodies avoid these problems by having a maturation temperature well in excess of the temperatures ever reached in the process and by maintaining an open pored and loosely bonded body.

Guide to the preparation of Raku clay bodies

As has been previously stated, clay is a very personal material and one with which the potter has to establish an intimate relationship. Raku clay in particular has to be an extension of his sensibilities – a material whose texture, plasticity, 'feel', consistency, etc. is working in total accord with the manipulations and concepts of the man.

With this in mind, it is clear that no formulations for clay bodies given here will satisfy the student of Raku for long. Soon he will begin to modify, then extensively change and finally totally re-conceive his material in the light of his own personality and experience.

Within this spectrum of personal experiment, however, the following general guidelines will be found applicable:

General percentage limits for components:
a Clays   50–70 per cent
b Grog or substitutes   30–45 per cent
c Fillers, fluxes, etc.   0–15 per cent
There are four main ways in which one may achieve a workable Raku clay body:
1 by buying a prepared Raku clay body from a ceramic supplier,
2 by modifying an existing plastic clay so as to make it suitable for Raku firing,
3 by compounding one's own clay body from dry industrially prepared materials,
4 by prospecting, digging and preparing one's own clay from nature.

1 Buying a ready-to-use Raku clay body

A number of the major ceramic suppliers now compound and sell coarse grained, thermal shock resistant bodies specifically for Raku firing; others sell bodies that although not advertised as being suitable for the process will, in fact, be quite satisfactory for it. Suppliers will be happy to advise on the suitability of their products.

Buying a commercial Raku clay body is certainly the quickest and easiest method of acquiring a working material. However, the true concerns, sensibilities and involvements that are the quintessence of Raku are utterly divorced from so doing. Those students of Raku who do use a commercial body for their first attempts rapidly discard it in favour of a personal one. As an art Raku works only when every factor reflects the ideas and sensitivities of personal involvement. This is most unlikely to be achieved when the primary material has been mass-produced by alien and uninvolved concepts of texture, 'feel', colour, plasticity, chemical composition and working qualities.

2 Modifying an existing clay body

A simple and popular method of developing a personal Raku clay is by the modification of a clay body that you already have available. A sensitive re-balance of the properties of any clay can make it usable for Raku.
This method necessitates:
a a simple assessment of the characteristics of the clay in hand,
b a comparison of these characteristics with those required for Raku,
c additions to the basic clay of those materials that will suitably modify its qualities.
The essential characteristics to be achieved are:
(i)   maturation temperature of 1200 °C or higher,
(ii) sufficient plasticity to make the clay workable,
(iii) a body which, in both raw and fired states, is extremely porous and open grained.

Most schools and potteries have available a supply of standard stoneware clay. Such a clay, or more groggy variations intended for large scale building or sculptural work, may be converted into a body which will withstand the stresses of Raku simply through the addition of more grog. The total grog content of the modified body should be about 40 per cent and its particle sizes should range from fine through medium to coarse in approximately equal amounts of each grade. The grog should be damped with a little water and left until this has been absorbed. Spread the grog, a handful at a time, on a wooden table or wedging board and knead and wedge it into the clay (plate 10). When the total amount of grog has been absorbed into the clay mass it must be wedged until homo-geneous. This may be observed visually by cutting through the mass with a potter's wire (plate 11). This extremely simple Raku body is suitable for a wide variety of forms and techniques.

The simple Raku body described above, while being perfectly acceptable, naturally lacks many refinements that the individual Rakuist might wish his material to possess. In pursuit of a more sophisticated body either an alternative basic clay or more complex modifications may be made. Each case will, of course, be individual and modifications will probably be made with particular physical qualities and forming techniques in mind.

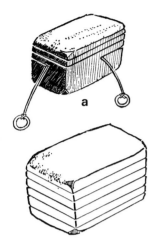

Fig. 2
Combining additive clay with basic mass

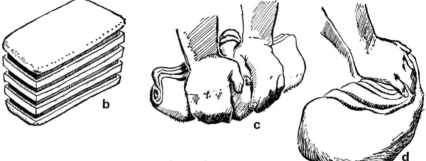

Method of combining additive clay to basic mass
1 Thoroughly wedge and knead basic clay mass. Beat into a rectangular form.
2 Repeat the above process with the additive clay.
3 Slice both masses of clay horizontally using a potter's wire (fig. 2a).
4 Intersperse layers of basic clay with layers of additive (fig. 2b and plate 12).
5 Wedge together by the *aramomi* (press wedge) method (fig. 2c and plate 13b). Then use the *nejimoni* (screw wedging) method (fig. 2d and plate 13a) to achieve total and even dispersal. Check by cutting through with wire: if streaks of the component layers are visible still more wedging is necessary (plate 14).

Analysis and suggested modifications
Do not expect to achieve a perfect result at the first attempt. Be prepared to make further admixtures in the light of your experience.

Remember to keep a careful note of the additions you make, since nothing is more frustrating than eventually arriving at an ideal body only to find it un-repeatable because you have forgotten what it contains.

3 Compounding a Raku body from dry commercially prepared materials

Precise requirements in a Raku body can best be satisfied through the 'dry compounding' method, in which each characteristic required of the body (such as colour, texture, resistance to thermal shock and plasticity) can be considered individually. This method does, however, presuppose the availability of storage facilities and a considerable financial outlay for the private potter since he has to have on hand a quite extensive range of bulk materials. The 'dry compounding' method is ideal for the professional potter or for the student with access to the facilities of a school or college department of ceramics.

Designing the clay body
While working within the general guidelines for Raku body composition a variety of materials can always be used to impart any given characteristic. Some of these alternatives will probably be undesirable (because of colour or because of the large amount needed). These will consequently be eliminated or substitutes found. Your final body composition will be the best compromise between those elements that will combine to produce exactly the kind of clay body you require for a particular style or working technique.

Characteristic	Material	Notes
a basic clay	1 stoneware clay 2 plastic fire clay 3 saggar clay 4 brick clay	these clays provide basic workability. Up to 60 per cent of stoneware clay may be used while even larger percentages of 2, 3 and 4 are often satisfactory
b texture, refractory nature and porous structure	1 saggar clay 2 fire clay 3 grog 4 washed sand 5 molochite 6 exfoliated vermiculite, calcined kyanite and sillimanite	 up to 50 per cent up to 40 per cent can substitute for part of the grog content can substitute for part of the grog when a white body or a fine throwing clay is required can substitute for part of the grog content
c plasticizers – increased green-strength	1 ball clay 2 bentonite 3 red earthenware clay	normally up to 20 per cent, but this can be increased if little or no stoneware clay is used highly efficient plasticizer. Limit up to about 3 per cent. (This will substitute for about 6 per cent ball clay)
d filler	flint	up to 5 per cent
e fired strength	1 kaolin 2 flint 3 talc 4 volcanic ash 5 feldspar	up to 30 per cent up to 5 per cent up to 20 per cent ⎫ up to 10 per cent ⎬ These act as body fluxes up to 10 per cent ⎭
f thermal shock resistance	1 β spodumene and other calcined lithium aluminum-silicates 2 grog 3 washed sand 4 fireclay 5 saggar clay 6 flint clay 7 brick clay 8 molochite 9 exfoliated vermiculite, calcined kyanite and sillimanite	(Negative expansion co-efficients.) Use small percentages

Characteristic	Material	Notes
g colour	RED	
	1 red earthenware clay	
	2 calcined yellow ochre	2–4 per cent
	3 red iron oxide	2–4 per cent
	4 brick clay	some brick clays impart a tan rather than red colour
	5 body stain	
	WHITE	
	Substitute white burning materials (such as kaolin, ball clay and molochite) for others	
	GREY	
	manganese dioxide	1–2 per cent
	ALL COLOURS	
	1 body stains	as recommended by manufacturers
	2 metallic oxides	will affect the colours of glazes used over them
	SPECKLES	
	1 granular manganese dioxide	$\frac{1}{2}$–2 per cent as desired
	2 iron spangles	$\frac{1}{2}$–2 per cent as desired
h water	Normally 20–30 per cent of total dry weight of materials. Percentages generally increase in direct proportion to the fineness of average particle size	

Suggested guidelines for Raku body compositions

1 *White Raku body for throwing*	per cent	2 *Off-white Raku body for pinched or carved forms*	per cent
stoneware clay	12		
ball clay	19	stoneware clay	24
kaolin	17	plastic fireclay	24
plastic fireclay	15	ball clay	12
grog, 36 mesh	19	grog, 30 mesh	12
grog, 30 mesh	18	washed sharp sand	28
water	26	water	20

3 Buff coarse Raku body for carved forms

	per cent
stoneware clay	22
plastic fireclay	20
ball clay	8
grog, 30 mesh	8
grog, 18 mesh	24
washed sharp sand	12
red earthenware clay	4
bentonite	2
	—
water	26

4 Raku body for general use

	per cent
stoneware clay	20
plastic fireclay	35
washed sand	35
talc	10
	—
water	20

5 White Raku body for general use

	per cent
stoneware clay	30
ball clay	14
feldspar	4
flint	4
grog, 36 mesh	3
grog, 28 mesh	20
fireclay	25
	—
water	26

6 Raku body for general use

	per cent
kaolin	17
ball clay	30
plastic fireclay	17
grog, 36 mesh	19
grog, 28 mesh	17
	—
water	25

7 Red or tan coarse Raku body for carved forms

	per cent
brick clay	40
washed sharp sand	30
stoneware clay	28
bentonite	2
	—
water	22

8 Buff Raku body for general use

	per cent
ball clay	20
plastic fireclay	30
mixed grog (all grades)	35
talc	10
earthenware clay	5
	—
water	25

9 Speckled grey-white body for fine forms

	per cent
saggar clay	15
ball clay	10
bentonite	2
kaolin	15
plastic fireclay	15
molochite	16
grog, 30 mesh	18
β spodumene	2
feldspar	5
exfoliated vermiculite	2
	—
iron spangles	2
water	26

Method of preparing the plastic body from dry materials
1 Weigh out dry materials.
2 Pass these together through a 20 mesh sieve to break down lumps.
3 Mix all materials together by hand in a large container.
4 Pass the mixed contents through a 20 mesh sieve twice to homogenize thoroughly. Mix by hand between these sievings.
5 Weigh water into a non-ferrous container and sprinkle the dry body materials on top of the water.
6 Cover container and allow materials to slake for four days.
7 Wedge thoroughly.
8 Wrap in polythene and store till required.
Stages 3 and 4 may be accomplished using a twin-shell dry blender if this equipment is available. Stages 2 to 5 may be accomplished in a mechanical clay mixer.

4 Prospecting, digging and preparing your own clay

The making of good Raku involves an understanding between yourself and all aspects of the process and materials developed to the point where it becomes a state of intuitive rapport. For this reason it is good to work initially with a limited number of materials, making an exhaustive study of their possibilities until their behaviour becomes an extension of yourself.

Undoubtedly the best starting point for acquiring a sound understanding of clay is by prospecting, testing, digging and preparing your own directly from the earth. This is often a very laborious and time-consuming process, but it is one which confronts you directly with the true nature, form and characteristic of clay.

Clay deposits occur in very many locations and in most parts of the world. Many of these are very small and would be an uneconomic proposition to mine for industrial purposes; many others are unsuitable due to their high content of sand and other impurities. These clays, however, can often form the basis of a highly satisfactory and personal Raku body and even a small deposit can be expected to supply a private studio for some time.

Secondary clays are of primary interest since they possess an unusually satisfactory degree of plasticity. These clays do occasionally occur on the surface but are more commonly to be found in seams or strata beneath the topsoil or other sedimentary deposits.

Prospecting
A consultation with the local librarian, geological office or the geology department of the nearest college or university will almost always give a precise location for local clay deposits. Look for seams of clay in places where deep incisions have been made into the earth, such as industrial diggings, excavations and river valleys. Here one can examine the various disclosed strata and search for a clay seam.

Natural clay may be recognized by its slick and sticky surface quality when wet and by its loose and crumbly nature when dry, in contrast with the resilience of other rocks and deposits. Usable clay deposits are most commonly red, tan, light to medium brown, white, grey or light green in colour. Small samples of possible deposits should be thoroughly damped down with water. If a plastic material results it is almost certainly a usable clay.

The majority of clay seams are contaminated by sand and iron, neither of which disqualify them from usefulness for Raku. The clay may, however, also contain considerable quantities of organic and carbonaceous matter which will have to be removed by screening if fine carving or throwing is contemplated. (If the clay is to be used for a fine production technique it is also necessary to test a sample for the presence of limestone particles, which are difficult to remove and anathema to most pottery processes.)

Raku, however, is a very flexible technique and many of its forms are well suited to even the most unrefined natural clays. Since Raku sets out to grasp the drama of change, random occurrence and natural process, the unpredictable effects produced by the impurities contained in the clay often make a desirable contribution to the work.

Digging

If tests on a sample of the clay show it to be suitable, proceed to dig a sizeable amount for use. Carefully clear away all surface matter and soil, leaving the seam clean and uncovered. Dig out the clay, using a small sharp spade and taking care to dig exclusively from the seam itself without polluting it with matter from its neighbouring strata. This is often more difficult to accomplish than would appear since clay seams are frequently shallow and deposited at an angle.

Preparing the clay

When sufficient clay has been gathered it can be slaked with water and kneaded together with sand for the production of coarse Raku forms. If a more refined clay is desired it should be broken into small pieces and dropped into an excess of water in a large non-ferrous container. The whole should be agitated by a mechanical blunger or, at intervals, by hand using a wooden paddle. Over a period of a few days the lumps will become dispersed and a clay slip will be produced. The slip should now be allowed to settle for a few days. The larger solid particles, such as coarse sand, will tend to settle at the bottom of the container below the clay layer, while humus and most of the organic matter will float on the surface of the water. The organic matter and the layer of water may now be siphoned off (fig. 3).

The deposit of more-or-less pure clay may next be drawn off and passed through a 20–28 mesh sieve to remove any larger foreign particles it may still contain. Alternatively, after the removal of the water the remainder of the contents of the container may be thoroughly remixed and passed together through a sieve to remove small stones and large sand particles. This will produce a clay that already contains a considerable percentage of fine sand.

The slip obtained after sieving should again be allowed to settle for a few days, surface water being siphoned off daily. When no further settlement occurs the thick slip is ready to be dried down to a workable consistency. This is most easily achieved by pouring the slip into dry plaster of Paris drying bats or dish-moulds (fig. 3). The plaster will absorb the excess water from the slip and cause the clay to stiffen to a plastic consistency.

At this stage grog or other desirable additions for a satisfactory Raku body should be made and the whole body thoroughly wedged.

Clay storage

Whenever a new batch of clay has been prepared by any method it is advantageous for it to be wedged and kneaded before storage; this not only assists in homogenizing the mixture but also serves to align the constituent clay particles and improve eventual workability.

After wedging the clay body should be wrapped in old damp sacking (preferably that which has been used before for this purpose) and the whole either wrapped in polythene sheeting or enclosed in an airtight container (fig. 4) and kept in a warm place for about a week. During this time its plasticity improves

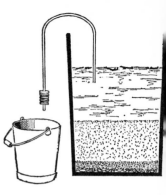

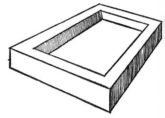

Fig. 3
Section through a clay
  settlement tank showing:
A Floating humus
B Water
C Clay
D Sand and small stones
The clay may be drawn off
  and dried in a plaster of
  Paris drying bat (**E**)

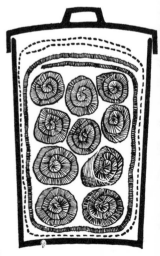

Fig. 4
Clay storage

considerably, due to the thorough saturation of all constituent clay particles and the development of colloidal gels within the clay as a result of bacterial action.

Reconstitution of waste clay

Clay often involves considerable work and effort in its production and preparation. Wastage is, consequently, to be avoided as much from practical standpoints as from concurrence with the Zen idea that 'scrap' clay is to be as highly regarded as the pot and should therefore be treated with equal concern. Any scrap Raku clay that is still in a plastic condition at the end of the day's work may be rewedged (on a plaster bat if it is very wet) and put in storage for use at a later date.

Rejected or broken but unfired forms, as well as scrap and trimmings which have dried out and become too hard to use, may be returned to a plastic state. These dry pieces should be pounded down into small fragments, placed into a container and sprinkled liberally with water. A damp sack should be used to cover the clay and the container should be sealed. Turn the pieces daily and re-sprinkle with water until they have absorbed sufficient moisture to be kneaded back into a plastic mass. This done, wedge thoroughly and store as normal.

4 Raku forming techniques

The traditional technique

The Raku family have, by tradition, been trained as sculptors and the forming techniques used in their work have consequently been drawn primarily from that art. By far their most common product has been the Raku *chawan* (Tea bowl) for use in the Tea Ceremony. These *chawan* are described by the present Raku Master as 'pieces of sculpture from which to drink Tea'. *Chawan* and other Tea Ceremony utensils (such as incense boxes, flower vases, food dishes and *sakazuki*) together with roof crest-tiles have accounted almost totally for the output of the fourteen generations of Raku Masters and have predominantly been formed by a carving-down process from a larger basic mass of stiff and semi-dry clay.

The carving-down technique requires great sensitivity and a high degree of manipulative dexterity and control. In Raku it also demands an ability to recognize and assimilate unforeseen elements that emerge as by-products of the process itself; thus an exciting synthesis between the initial idea and the evolving form can be achieved.

In Western pottery carving is often used for surface decoration but is seldom employed for the production of the form itself. Quite apart from being the indispensable method of producing traditional style *chawan*, carving can be extended to cover a whole range of other forms and, since it poses different problems of stress and structure from those that condition most pottery formed from soft plastic clay, carved forms can offer a new expressive dimension.

The classical Raku *chawan* is an exciting sculptural object because its many practical requirements demand creativity in depth in order to avoid mere repetition. The *chawan* form has, in fact, become so perfectly evolved that most students and makers of Raku find themselves periodically drawn back to it as a test of skill and a means of evaluating their developing sensibilities to the art. (As such, it serves as a central point of reference, even to Rakuists untrained in the subtleties of the traditional forms.)

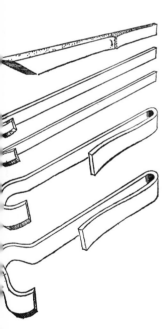

Fig. 5
Traditional types of Raku clay carving tools which can be made quite easily by bending and grinding lengths of suitable metal

The traditional Raku *chawan* is carved from a thick basic form, which is itself most easily achieved by pinching out a ball of clay between the thumb and fingers of one hand while supporting the whole rounded form in the other (fig. 6a).

The overall thickness of the basic form has to be sufficiently great to contain within itself whatever modulations of form are to be required of the bowl. The initial 'dome' shape from which the bowl is cut is always made extra thick at the base to allow a foot-ring to be carved (fig. 6b).

A number of basic forms are made and are then turned upside down on a flat board and allowed to dry for one day or until the clay is sufficiently stiff to be handled without fear of distortion. The inside of the 'dome' form is damped with a little water and work is started on the exterior by shaving the base of the bowl flat and the walls regular in profile (fig. 6c).

A foot-ring is carved from the flat base (fig. 6d). This has to be tested for a comfortable 'feel' when resting in the palm of the hand. The interior of the form should be damped at regular intervals.

The main characteristics of the exterior form of the bowl are achieved by carving away surplus clay (fig. 6e) until the desired modulations are present. The form must be constantly tested for a good relationship to the hands.

When the main character of the exterior form is completed the shape of the lip can be cut (fig. 6f). This normally rises and falls rhythmically to form a number of *gaku* (peaks or hills). The interior of the form should now be comparatively soft from the several dampings it has received and can easily be carved as required. The approach to the drinking point on the rim of the bowl is the most important interior feature.

When carving the interior form it is necessary to proceed with great precaution, constantly supporting the walls from the outside against the pressure from the cutting tool on the inside (fig. 6g). Check frequently the thickness of the clay that remains. The ideal form has approximately the same thickness at all points.

Some practical problems

The only limitations that need be placed on a Raku form are those that govern 'what will work'.

The piece has to be placed into, and removed from, a small red-hot kiln with a pair of tongs. It follows that the piece must be within the size limitations of the kiln to be used and not be so heavy as to be unmanageable. The design of the kiln also needs to be related to the form of the wares to be fired, in that one usually snatches the pot from a top-loading kiln by gripping it with the tongs at a single point at its lip or neck – these, therefore, have to be sufficiently strong to withstand this treatment. Front-loading kilns, on the other hand, frequently allow one to grasp the pot around its belly, which is less likely to damage the form and unlikely to damage the lip. It is also important to remember that the process of introducing and withdrawing the piece from the kiln can subject the potter, as well as the pot, to a considerable heat ordeal. Under such circumstances it is desirable to have a piece which is easy to grasp. Forms which are difficult to lift with the tongs are certainly to be avoided.

If a piece fails to satisfy any of these practical requirements we can safely say that it is ill-conceived in spite of any aesthetic merits. Zen accepts no division between day-to-day practicality and aesthetic activity. In Raku also practical considerations must be indivisible from aesthetic ones.

Apart from problems of size and ease of handling the piece, there are two other practical factors which may influence the design of the form itself and the

Fig. 6
Traditional method of making a Raku *chawan*

a

b

d

e

technique by which it is made. Both of these are associated with the tremendous stresses set up within the form by the severe thermal shock to which the Raku piece is subjected upon being placed into, and withdrawn from, the kiln. The strains of rapid and possibly uneven expansion and contraction will be experienced in all parts of the form. These may well result in splits, cracks or breakage at any points of weakness. Nature seems to exert her own kind of censorship in Raku and slovenly workmanship or ill-resolved forms are frequently rejected when offered to the test by fire. Particularly vulnerable are such structural weaknesses as joins or lutes. The carving technique of classical Raku avoids this problem, but frequently we wish to construct forms from a number of parts. When doing so it is vital that the utmost attention be given to the quality of the joins. As far as is possible all the parts to be joined together should have the same moisture content, but of course this is not always possible. If parts of differing degrees of dampness are joined it is important that the moisture content of the whole piece is allowed to equalize before it is put to dry. The most satisfactory method of working under these circumstances is to score thoroughly all the surfaces to be joined with a pin, nail or knife and work a little slurry (some of the same Raku body mixed with an excess of water so that it is like thick cream) into these surfaces. The open nature of Raku clay quickly absorbs this slurry and the additional softness of the clay assists in achieving a perfect join. The two soft parts must be pressed firmly together and worked into one another so well that any semblance of a joint or weakness is eliminated. When the forming of the piece is complete the whole should be lightly damped and wrapped in polythene for a few days. This allows the moisture within all parts of the piece to equalize and thereby eliminates uneven drying strains.

A second category of forms that tend to suffer an unduly large number of casualties are those with very narrow necks or openings, such as bottles, particularly Raku bottles thrown on the potter's wheel. The risk of dunting may be reduced by the provision of wider necks or by having more than one opening. Thrown forms that have a sudden change of direction within the planes of the form are also common kiln casualties. Both these and bottle forms favour a slower cooling than is usual after being withdrawn from the glaze kiln – long periods in the secondary reduction tank are ideal.

It is perhaps against the spirit of Raku to write at any length about the many other problems which may be encountered, since the only problems which are really meaningful are those which you yourself raise as a result of practical experience. It is important always to remember that the way forward is through solving these problems. When a pot breaks or a certain design of kiln fires unevenly or a glaze fails to melt satisfactorily do not allow yourself to avoid discovering why it happened, for understanding the mishap is an opportunity for enlarging your understanding of Raku.

Gradually, after you have participated and been involved in the Raku process a few times, you will find that your personal experience modifies the forms you make, the materials you use and your techniques of glazing and firing.

Creating and solving your own problems will develop your work along individual and distinctive lines, yet will simultaneously bring you closer to the point where your personal expression becomes intuitively infused with an understanding of every aspect of the process. It is from this synthesis that good Raku comes.

Other methods of forming Raku

Throwing
Raku may be very satisfactorily thrown on a potter's wheel. Clay bodies specially designed for this technique and having a less coarse texture than for carving should be used. The comparative lack of plasticity that even these Raku throwing bodies have compared with common throwing clays demand that you work quickly and decisively. Attempts to take too many 'pulls' up the walls of a form will cause it to tear or collapse. If a further 'pull' is essential on any form which already seems to have reached the limits of its endurance it is advisable to remove the bat from the wheel with the pot still attached and allow the form to stiffen somewhat before replacing the bat and completing the piece.

Paddling
Basic Raku forms can be satisfactorily wheel thrown and, after they have stiffened somewhat, they can be modified into rather less predictable shapes by beating them with a flat piece of wood known as a 'paddle'. Most square Raku forms are produced in this way. The surfaces of paddles may be carved so as to impart a low relief decoration to the clay form.

Pinching and joining
Simple bowl forms can be made by pinching out a small ball of clay between the fingers and thumb. With practice forms of remarkable control and sensitivity can be achieved. Two such forms can be carefully joined lip-to-lip to make simple bottle forms. These may be further refined by paddling or carving.

Slab building
Pots and small sculptural constructions can be produced using the common slab building technique. Extra care needs to be taken in preparing and making the joins so that any semblance of weakness is eliminated. It is also essential that the whole form be lightly damped and wrapped in polythene sheeting for several days so that the moisture content in all parts of the form may equalize.

Press moulding
Raku dishes and tiles can be made by pressing rolled-out slabs of clay into plaster of Paris or bisque-fired clay moulds or by pressing the clay directly on to some interesting textural surface (such as weather-beaten wooden boards, tree bark, straw matting) and then shaping by hand.

Casting
Slip casting might at first sight seem to violate the basic aesthetic propositions of Raku but, since one often learns as much by breaking aesthetic rules as by applying them, you may wish to attempt it. A slip based on low-shrinkage and thermal shock resistant materials (such as the lithium group) would seem to be the most appropriate.

Mixed media constructions
Constructions incorporating elements such as metals, wire and glass make an interesting contrast to the more traditional type of wares. Metals may be incorporated into the pieces when dry (making an allowance for clay shrinkage) and bonded to the clay at a later stage with glaze. Alternatively, the metals and glass can be added with the glaze to the bisque-fired form.

   All the above processes can, of course, be combined with others to produce a wide and rich variety of forming techniques.

5 Raku aesthetics

Potters and pottery receive comparatively little attention from aestheticians and writers on the philosophy of art. This is in itself surprising but may, in some measure, be accounted for by the fact that pottery in the West has traditionally been considered to be an 'applied art' and therefore inferior to such 'pure' and 'high art' activities as painting and sculpture. Also, the ceramic arts in the West have not been practised by the greatest creative geniuses; had Donatello, Raphael, Leonardo, Rembrandt and Vermeer, for example, been potters perhaps the art would occupy a much higher and more sympathetic place in our critical estimations. It follows that the forms which have been produced by our potters have not become cornerstones of our culture and thereby seminal to our thinking and attitudes to life and art. In the Far East, and particularly in Japan, the situation is almost the reverse. Koetsu, Chojiro, Nonko, Ninsei and Ogata Kenzan, to mention but a few of the famous names, together with generations of great but anonymous potters, have raised the status of the ceramic arts in popular and critical esteem to that of the sublime art which, more than any other, is emblematic of the tastes, aesthetic sensibilities and spirit of the Japanese people.

The Tea Ceremony proved to be the vehicle that stimulated the highest levels of attainment in many aspects of Japanese life. It was certainly thanks to the cult of Teaism that Raku owed its development and prestige. The classic forms of Raku were developed by the great Tea Master Sen-no-Rikyu and Chojiro, the first generation of Raku, as a cooperative venture in creating, specially for *Cha-no-yu*, a ceramic ware that was permeated through and through with the highly sophisticated spirit of *wabi*. The *Wabi-no-Cha-no-yu* (austere Teaism) was built on the two Zen aesthetic foundations of *wabi* and *sabi*. *Wabi* is concerned with a belief that the highest appreciation of beauty is the perception of beauty in things quiet, simple and imperfect, while the highest achievement of beauty lies in creating works that have thrown off the pose and shackles of being self-conscious art objects and exist unostentatiously as functional objects whose greatest aesthetic claims are their sense of absolute suitability for their purpose and their total accordance with nature and natural processes. *Sabi*, on the other hand, means to be mellowed and beautified by age and use. New objects tend to be 'loud' and assertive and the cult of *sabi* prefers the patina that common use gives to an object, making it quiet and reticent. This is of course linked to the Zen idea that life experiences are part of the process of achieving enlightenment (becoming beautiful).

Since there is so little aesthetic evaluation of pottery in the West, perhaps it would be useful to look briefly at some of the more fundamental devices* that the synthesis of Chojiro's sculptural genius with Rikyu's Tea concept evolved for the embodiment of *wabi* suitability. Although you may not wish to make Raku in the traditional style, some attention to traditional wares still serves to sharpen sensitivities and stimulate thinking.

Raku bowls have been created exclusively for the drinking of powder tea and any attempt to divorce the object from its practical purpose (for instance, by placing it in a museum) is inevitably detrimental both to the bowl itself and to our appreciation of it. Raku bowls can only be truly appreciated through use.

The specific thermal qualities of clay used for Raku *chawan* are of aesthetic importance. Raku bodies are refractory in nature and bad conductors of heat.

---

* These were added to after the death of Rikyu as the result of similar cooperative efforts between Sen Sotan and Raku Masters, Sokei, Jokei and Nonko.

This serves the practical purpose of keeping the tea warm as long as is necessary for the *Cha-no-yu* formalities. Its second purpose is to impart a pleasant but non-extreme sensation to the hands when the bowl is held.

The range of shapes for Raku *chawan* has also been evolved with thermal considerations in mind. In this case they have been coupled with prevailing seasonal characteristics to produce what are known as the 'seasonal modes of *chawan*'.

Japanese winters are cold and the *sukiya* (Tea house) particularly makes comparatively little provision for providing warmth. In consequence the tea itself requires maximum thermal insulation to protect it against the cold. Winter mode bowls are therefore high-walled and wrap in, around and over the tea as much as possible so that its heat shall not be dissipated by the atmosphere.

Conversely, summer Tea Ceremonies take place when the air is very warm and it becomes unnecessary to provide measures for keeping the tea warm. This results in *chawan* of the summer mode being low, wide and shallow in design and having qualities of gaiety and colour, whereas the bowls of the winter mode are severe, dark and sombre in atmosphere.

Between these two extremes is a range of shapes and colours which relate to every variation of season and even allow for ceremonies conducted at special times of day.

The exterior profile shapes of the *chawan* are determined by a number of factors. Stability is very important. The bowl must be able to stand confidently on its foot when placed on the *tatami* – any sense of anxiety over its stability would disturb the *Cha-no-yu* atmosphere. (Indeed this is one of the factors in which a number of Koetsu's *chawan* demonstrate their lesser 'suitability for Tea' than the products of the *Hon-gama* wares.) However, the *chawan* is primarily intended to be held in the hands and it is the way it feels and how it fits the hands when held and turned and tipped to drink that is the main concern of the potter. The bowl must be capable of sitting comfortably in the palm of the left hand and feel easy, pleasant and comfortable while there. The winter modes of *chawan*, having higher walls (and consequently tending towards less stability) are modelled with particular emphasis on a low centre of gravity.

The *chawan* is always presented to the guest with the 'front' of the bowl facing him. Before drinking the bowl has to be turned so that the drinking point on the lip (which is opposite the 'front') is brought into the appropriate position and the 'front' thereby directed back towards the host. This turning process is more comfortably and easily accomplished if the exterior of the bowl is modelled with subtle modulations to assist in this, particularly important on the bowl's left side.

Of the numerous aesthetic requirements of Raku three of the most important (all relating to Zen concepts) deserve mention:

Zangurishita is concerned with the possession of an agreeable tactile quality with an emphasis on slight roughness. There is also a desire for textural variation within the piece. As the bowl is turned in the hands it should offer a tactile 'happening'. When one holds a natural object, such as a rock, its surface qualities differ from point to point in colour, gloss, texture, tone and general sensation. The Raku bowl is also expected to present a similar rich variety of subtle sensation-enriching experiences. Zen expects us to develop 'awareness' in the light of the immediacy of incoming experience; the Raku bowl must be a veritable treasure house of tactile and visual experiences.

Tedori is an aesthetic expression of the existence of a direct relationship between what is actual and what is apparent. If a certain bowl visually gives the appearance of being massive, dense and heavy when placed before us on the *tatami* then we can expect it to feel exactly that way when lifted and held in the hands. Like-

Fig. 7

wise, a bowl that appears light and buoyant visually must communicate a similar experience when lifted. Generally, however, a feeling of moderateness is considered most desirable in terms of weight, as in all things connected with Raku.

Keshiki is a desire for the appearance of a faint dampness and softness about the glaze and the kinds of colour variation that dampness can impart. Raku deteriorates as an experience when it is allowed to dry out completely and for this reason *chawan* in the collections of museums are frequently disappointing to handle. The qualities of touch, sound and *tedori* are distorted. Also, of course, if the appearance of dampness is built into the bowls' glazes then damp they should be. In Japan all Raku bowls are used at regular intervals to retain this quality. (Iga and Bizen wares also, both frequently used as *Cha-no-yu* utensils, should not be allowed to dry out completely.)

The interior forms of Raku *chawan* are as sculptural and definitively conceived as their exteriors. The interior carving has four main features (fig. 7). *Cha-no-yu* makes use of the powdered style of tea adopted in Japan from the Chinese Sung period. Powder tea for *Cha-no-yu* is made from the very best shooting tea leaves from the old bushes. After picking the leaves are steamed, cured and pulverized into a fine powder. The tea is made by adding hot water to the powder tea in the *chawan* itself and by kneading *koicha* (thick tea, the first tea course in *Cha-no-yu*) or whisking *usucha* (thin tea, the second tea course in *Cha-no-yu*) into a homogeneous and deliciously fragrant beverage with a bamboo whisk (*chasen*).

Chajin favour a crazed or cracked glaze on *chawan* (the motion of the *chasen* produces a harsh hard note on uncracked glazes) – this also is related to the concept of softness in sound.

There is normally a gap in the ridge or spiral (B) or it decreases in height immediately below the point on the rim that is used for drinking, thus allowing the tea to flow gently to the mouth without having to mount and be partly trapped behind the ridge. There is only one drinking point on a Tea bowl: this is smooth and makes pleasant contact with the lips and is situated directly opposite the front or decorated part of the bowl. Some Raku bowls have no obviously decorated front and in these cases the front is normally that part of the bowl which is scarred by the mark which the tongs leave in the soft glaze when it is removed from the kiln.

At the base of the inside of the bowl (A) can be seen a second spiral which sweeps gently down into a shallow depression at the lowest point. This is known as the *cha-damari* or tea pool. This spiral is designed to feed down any last drops of tea that remain so that they may gather as naturally as rainwater in the depression of a rock.

The top lip of the bowl is not flat (fig. 7), but rises and falls in a series of waves known as *gaku* (or hills). There are usually three, five or seven *gaku*. Besides adding variety and naturalness to the bowl, they also make reference back to the mountains rising through the clouds (a common subject in Chinese Ch'an Buddhist paintings of the Sung period), which were used as vehicles for meditation by the monks, and also to the stones of the rock gardens of the Zen monasteries laid down during the Muromanchi period for the same purpose.

The colours of Raku bowls are limited to black or brown–black (*kuro*), red (*aka*), white (*shiro*) and green (*ao*). This range has been carefully chosen for its pleasant relationship to the beautiful green of powder tea, and the bowls must be seen when containing tea to fully appreciate the colour qualities of Raku glazing. These colours are also related to the seasonal shapes and help to create a wider range of moods than is possible from shape alone. In *Cha-no-yu* every detail must be felt to be totally suitable for the particular occasion.

There are numerous other factors that contribute to the making and the full appreciation of classical Raku. I have attempted here simply to describe enough to demonstrate that every factor in the design of Raku is considered and is purposeful; but perhaps the greatest achievement of the Raku has been their ability to embody all these many practical and aesthetic requirements into forms that speak to us predominantly of ease, naturalness and unostentatious simplicity. Indeed, many early Western visitors to Japan described the Raku wares as 'crudely made and quite without artifice'. This, of course, was not intended as praise, but in their simple responses they saw the bowls exactly as Rikyu had envisaged them. The painstaking application of skill to concept had produced forms that exuded simple naturalness. The simple rusticity that is so fundamental to Rikyu's *Wabi-no-Cha-no-yu* has a highly evolved and subtle superstructure, which largely explains its unerring sense of harmony and aesthetic brilliance.

6 Decorative processes

The best Raku has a sense of moderateness and restraint in all its aspects. The form is always a sculptural experience, but never a vulgar display of the artist's technical ability. The glazes complement the form, but never overpower it, and any applied decoration makes quiet reference to the mood or season for which the bowl is intended, but never ostentatiously overshadows the other elements with a virtuoso performance of decorative skill – such is considered to be '*mu cha*' (not Tea).

In classical Raku applied decoration is used for the two main purposes of denoting the fronts of Tea bowls and assisting to create a mood of lighthearted gaiety in the implements used for summer Tea Ceremonies.

One of the most exciting elements in the art of making Raku arises out of the face-to-face confrontation of the controlled and intentional with the chance modifications that are brought about by the nature of the process. Raku firing eliminates mere complacent predictability and forces a dramatic compromise between intent and the chance phenomena of natural occurrence. Consequently, the spirit of Raku demands a style of applied decoration that is swift, has vitality, will not conflict with the natural 'signature' of the process and which is carried out in a way that is fundamentally consistent with the nature of the brush, tool, pigment or material used.

Brushwork

Brushwork decoration is one of the most famous features of Oriental ceramics. It is at its best in simple, vigorous treatment. The ceramic products of Sung China, the Korean Yi dynasty, the Japanese Momoyama and early Edo periods as well as Islamic wares are all worthy of attention in this respect, as are the paintings of Southern Sung China's Ch'an sect and Japan's own Zen Buddhist calligraphers.

Of all the decorative processes applicable to Raku, brushwork demands most physical control, mental discipline, and aesthetic sensitivity.

Gather together a collection of brushes (fig. 8) and test all the possibilities and variations obtainable with each type. Try making your own brushes from grass, hair or the crushed ends of twigs. The marks from these are usually looser and

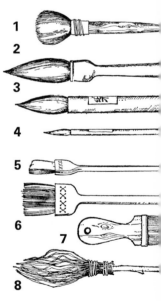

Fig. 8
Brushes commonly used for decorating and glazing Raku:
1 Glazing mop
2, 3 and 4 *Fude* types
5, 6 and 7 *Hake* types
8 *Hakeme* type

more idiosyncratic than those from bought brushes and consequently they make a useful extension to your range. Treat your brushes, whether bought or self-made, with respect, keep them clean and smooth them into shape after use.

The simplest and most satisfactory materials for Raku painted decoration techniques are clay slips and natural earths. Most varieties of natural earth can be used and they should be finely ground and mixed with sufficient water to produce a thin creamy liquid of a consistency that is suitable for brushing. Yellow ochre is the most commonly used earth colour in Raku and gives a rich red-brown when fired.

The prepared oxides of metals, such as are used to impart colour to ceramic glazes, may also be used for brushwork decoration. The oxide of each metal fires to a distinctive colour under a glaze: cobalt oxide, for example, gives a strong blue colour, iron a rich brown and tin oxide white. (The colour of the oxide in its raw state does not necessarily resemble its fired colour.) Metallic oxides tend to be excessively strong in an undiluted state and for brushwork decoration are best mixed into a little thin white clay slip. Cobalt and copper particularly need to be diluted in this way.

Clay slips for brushwork can be made from any clay by mixing with water until a paint-like liquid is obtained. Clay slips will fire to the same colour as the clay from which they were made. Coloured slips can be produced by adding small percentages of the appropriate metallic oxide. Earth or slip decoration should be applied to the form before the bisque firing and ideally at the point when the form is stiff but not yet fully dry.

The consistency of all these materials should be adjusted to suit individual preferences, the type of brush being used and the effect desired. Assess the decorative needs of the form before beginning to paint on it. Do not apply decoration at all unless it will make a positive contribution to the overall concept and atmosphere of the piece.

Try to be decisive and commit yourself to a strong mark. If you do not like the mark you have made do not compromise your principles by trying to 'touch it up'. The mark you make is after all a clear indication of the quality of your thought and dexterity; by falsifying it you succeed only in deluding yourself. Our aim must be to achieve the perfect mark – the physical achievement of the finest idea.

Splashed decoration

All the materials mentioned above for use in brushwork decoration can, of course, be applied in other ways to obtain different decorative effects. Splashed and dripped decoration is popular among a number of Rakuists since it seems to relate well to the chance effects achieved by the secondary reduction process. Splashed and dripped decoration, particularly if applied with restraint, conjures up associations with nature which also seem to make the technique consistent with the Tea aesthetic.

Thicker slips can be used in splashed decoration on freshly made Raku forms if a rough textural effect is required in addition to colour.

Sgraffito and combed decoration

Decorative motifs may be incised directly into the pot form with a pointed tool. This type of decoration is most effective when combined with a contrasting colour. Paint a thick layer of slip on to the damp form with a *hake* brush and allow it to stiffen. The sgraffito decoration may then be drawn through the layer of slip, disclosing the contrasting colour that lies beneath.

Alternatively, interesting combed effects can be achieved from using a home-made wooden *kushi* (fig. 9) on the semi-dry pot or through a layer of slip. (Ordinary hair combs and saw blades can also be used for this effect.)

Mishima (inlay)

The decorative technique known as *mishima* also makes use of a colour contrast, achieved either through the use of a slip of different colour to that of the form or through the use of two clays of contrasting colour.

The decorative motifs are first cut into the walls of the form with a pointed tool or fine gouge, after which these incisions are either filled with a thick slip or packed with a plastic clay of similar moisture content to that of the form itself. When the form and its inlay have dried the surface is scraped down with a sharp tool to reveal the original motif rendered as a clear two-tone image.

Paddled or impressed decoration

The predictable geometry of wheel-thrown Raku forms may be modified by being beaten into irregular forms with a shaped piece of wood known as a 'paddle' (fig. 9). This distortion of the form is effected when the pot has dried enough to be handled freely, yet still plastic enough to be paddled without serious cracks opening up in the walls and base. The marks left by the paddle during this process are evidence of the forces that created the piece and can be retained to decorative effect.

An extension of this effect may be achieved through the use of special paddles, the surfaces of which have been textured or cut into relief patterns which will leave a decorative impression in the clay.

Relief stamps can be cut out of wooden blocks or carved into blocks of plaster of Paris and also used to create relief effects on Raku forms.

Natural organic matter, such as straw, small twigs or rice, can be pressed into the outer surfaces of pieces while still soft. These can either be removed immediately or left impressed in the form to burn away during the bisque firing.

Any object made of metal or other non-organic material may be used to give surface decoration and texture to the soft Raku form. The impressions of man-made and machine parts coupled with the natural and unpredictable glaze effects can, on occasions, produce highly stimulating results.

Since it is very popular to leave parts of the exterior of Raku pieces unglazed in order that they may take up carbon during secondary reduction and provide an effective colour and matt textural foil to the glazed areas, the type of textural decoration described above can be used to heighten this contrast.

Fig. 9
Tools for applying surface decoration to the Raku form:
A *Kushi* for combing patterns into the soft form
B Roller stamp
C Carved paddle for modifying thrown forms
D Bamboo slip trailer

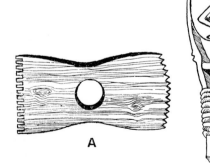
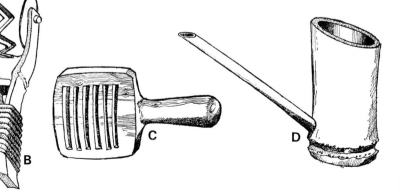

7 Drying, bisque firing and carbon shadow decoration

On completion of the forming stage it is particularly valuable in the Raku process to stop and, very deliberately, take stock of what you have done, assessing the product objectively as well as subjectively. It is all too easy to forge ahead in the full flush of creative excitement and neglect the conscious assimilation of what has been achieved. Inevitably, we work simultaneously on a number of levels; each of the senses arrives at awareness through its part in the whole activity and reacts in its own way. Some of these perceptions and the reactions they trigger off are conscious and controlled, others are unconscious and intuitive.

Perhaps the most difficult requirement of Raku is the achievement of that critical balance between all its elements so that no single element appears to stand forward from the rest. This can only be achieved through a detailed assessment of developments at each stage of the process and considered counterbalance in the next.

Look carefully into every aspect of your piece, familiarize yourself with the relationship that each element has to the others. Allow your mind time to fully understand what has been made, for this is an indispensable prelude to achieving balance and harmony between the form and the forthcoming processes of decoration and glazing.

Finally, be discriminating. Not every form you make will have excellence. Set a high standard for yourself which is in keeping with the art you study and reject those pieces which are below your creative capabilities.

Drying

After all forming and green ware decoration of the pot is complete it must be carefully and thoroughly dried before receiving its first, or bisque, firing.

The most important factor in the drying of Raku is that it should proceed uniformly and that all parts of the piece should dry at the same rate. During drying the form loses physically combined water (alternatively called water of plasticity or pore water) and shrinks in size. If parts of the form dry more rapidly than others there is a tendency for stresses to be set up in the form which results in cracks, faults or lines of weakness. Although these may be invisible at this time they commonly cause dunting or shattering when the piece undergoes the severe thermal shocks of Raku glaze firing.

Raku forms may be satisfactorily air dried by being left to stand in a warm, dry atmosphere. Work dried in this way should be placed on a shelf made of narrow wooden slats or expanded metal which allows the air to reach the base of the form (fig. 10). When the pots have dried somewhat they should be turned upside-down and remain resting on their lip until drying is complete.

Air drying, while being an almost foolproof method, does take several days and for this reason artificial means of accelerating the process are often employed. Many potteries have gas-fired or electric drying cabinets as part of their standard equipment and these may be used satisfactorily.

Pieces may also be dried by standing them in a warm kiln for a few minutes, after which they should be removed and allowed to stand in the air for a while. This process may be repeated a number of times.

One of the best ways of drying Raku quickly is to stand pieces on the warm fire-box cover or on the roof of the air supply tunnel of a fuel burning kiln that is in the process of being fired. The pots should stand in an upright position and should be turned around at regular intervals (fig. 10).

Clay normally changes colour as it dries; clay that is still damp feels colder than clay that is thoroughly dry. While these are good tests for the progress of air drying they are, for obvious reasons, less satisfactory in determining the dryness of wares that are being artificially dried. Pots must be left until there is no question as to their dryness before they are bisque fired.

Fig. 10
The two most satisfactory
  methods of drying Raku
  wares: (top) the inverted
  forms are slowly air dried
  on a slatted wooden shelf;
  (bottom) the wares are
  dried around a fuel burning
  kiln

Bisque firing

Traditional Raku is always bisque fired before being glazed. It is possible, however, to glaze and fire pieces in the green state. A special clay body and modified firing technique is used for this type of glazing. The glazing of other Raku bodies in a green state is not recommended and should not in any case be attempted without taking special precautions such as facial protection.

The purpose of the bisque fire is to bring about a chemical change in the clay. No matter how carefully a form is dried only physically combined water is removed. As can be seen from the chemical formula of clay, water is one of the substances that it contains in a chemical bond. This bond can be broken and the chemically combined water given off through the application of heat. The bisque fire firstly drives off any traces of physically combined water that the form may still contain and then goes on slowly to raise the temperature to the point where the chemically bonded water is released. This chemical change converts the clay to a rigid and stable material which the application of water will not reverse into a plastic material.

All physically held water will be removed between the temperatures of 100°C and 200°C, while the release of water from the clay molecule will be effected between 350°C and 700°C. It is essential that bisque firing is begun extremely slowly and is built up very gradually until all water has been removed. An excessive rate of temperature rise during bisqueing will cause shattering of the wares being fired.

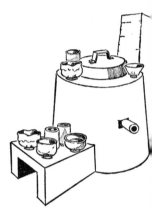

Although clay is converted to an irreversibly stable substance as a result of being fired it must be remembered that Raku is intended to be 'soft' in all its characteristics and this includes the actual mechanical strength of the material. Consequently Raku is never fired to the higher temperatures which would result in a material of greater physical strength and hardness. Raku is usually bisque fired to between 850–900°C, although certain bodies require the additional strength that is obtained from the formation of mullite between 955–1010°C. But the real strength of any Raku piece must come from a well designed, well engineered and resolved form rather than from the intrinsic fired strength of the material.

Bisque firing may be carried out in the Raku kiln itself, but since the capacity of its firing chamber is usually very small it is only possible to bisque three or four pieces at any one time. For this reason it is normal to build a separate bisqueing kiln of similar design but of larger proportions. If an extended period of work in the Raku process is contemplated this kiln may be built in addition to the glazing kiln. Alternatively, a bisque kiln may be made for the first firing of a considerable number of wares after which it can be dismantled and the bricks reused to construct the glazing kiln.

The main component of the bisque kiln is the firing chamber. This consists of a cylindrical, fireproof lidded box known as a saggar. The saggar is either wheel thrown or slab built from black Raku clay or saggar clay to a thickness of half an inch. (In Japan rice hull is mixed with the clay and thus serves to increase the

Fig. 11
Saggar design for bisque
  firing

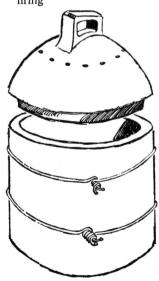

Fig. 12
Method of packing wares into
the saggar for the bisque
firing

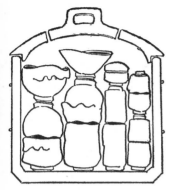

porosity of the saggar, which facilitates increased heat penetration.) The saggar is covered with a fitting domed lid surmounted with a handle. The lid should be perforated with a few holes about the diameter of a pencil.

Besides acting as a container for the wares to be fired, the main purpose of the saggar is to protect them from the direct effects of the fire and to promote equalization of the temperature. The saggar itself must be fired to about 1000 °C before it is used in the bisque kiln.

Surrounding the saggar (fig. 11) is a brick wall, constructed from common building bricks. The wall should rise some two bricks above the highest point of the domed lid. The gap left between the saggar and the inside of the brick wall should be some 2½ in. at the top of the saggar and 3½ in. at its base. Gaps are left between the bricks on the foundation layer of the kiln wall to provide air intake for fuel combustion. The saggar stands in the kiln upon three firebricks or rests on three or four steel bars built into the kiln walls.

No fireclay need be used in the construction of the brick kiln wall but after its completion any gaps between the bricks (except on the foundation layer) should be plugged with mud or thick clay waste or slurry.

The wares for bisque firing, which must be thoroughly dry, are packed into the saggar (fig. 12). Heavier pieces are stacked at the bottom of the saggar and the lighter pieces arranged on top of them. Larger forms may have smaller pieces packed inside them, although this is not advisable if carbon shadows are required as part of the decoration on those smaller pieces and it is the intention to achieve this through the 'standard kiln method' (see page 41).

For reasons of maximum economy the saggar may be packed with as many pots as it will contain.

The kiln is lit at the bottom using oil-soaked rag and wood or some convenient substitute. (A metal drum containing a few gallons of discarded automobile sump oil is a valuable asset. Split timber can be soaked in this oil for a few days, after which it generates considerable heat for use in wood-burning kilns and for general kiln lighting. The oil drum must not, of course, be situated near the kiln.)

When the kindling wood is burning briskly in the kiln a little coke may be added from the top. (The domed lid of the saggar ensures that it is directed downwards.) When this, too, is well ignited the kiln may be filled with coke to the level indicated in the diagram (fig. 13). Initial ignition may also be assisted by a forced air supply from a bellows or air pump.

The rise in temperature in this type of kiln is very gradual at first, becoming rather faster after a few hours. This is the ideal pattern for a temperature curve during bisque firing.

The kiln must be checked at regular intervals to ensure that the temperature is not rising too rapidly. Should it do so alternate air supply gaps between the bricks in the kiln's foundation layer may be closed with mud or slurry. Additional temperature control may be effected by covering the kiln mouth with a lid, either totally or in part as the situation demands.

The temperature in the saggar should reach a red heat (850–950 °C) over a period of about six hours. In Japan this firing period is extended to ten hours.

Variations of the wood-burning Raku glaze kiln may also be used for bisqueing, but a great deal of work is involved in stoking while the coke-burning bisque kiln requires only occasional attention.

Gas and electric kilns are also suitable, if less authentic, for bisque firing. No saggar is required and the wares are dried and packed in the normal manner for bisque firing. As with the fuel-burning kilns, the rise in temperature must be very slow for the first 500 °C, after which it may be accelerated until the required temperature has been reached.

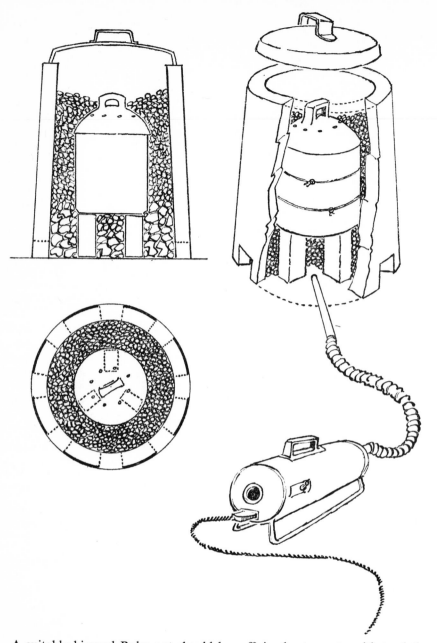

Fig. 13
Design of kiln for bisque
    firing: the use of some form
    of air blower to assist in
    lighting the kiln is optional

A suitably bisqued Raku pot should be sufficiently strong to withstand the handling with tongs that it is to receive and the pores of the body should be open and generally in a very porous and non-vitrified state. Should pots prove to be insufficiently strong the bisqueing temperature for the particular body you are using will have to be raised somewhat in future firings. On the other hand, if the pots have become dense during firing the kiln was fired to much too high a temperature. (A state of semi-vitrification is most unlikely to occur with a Raku body in the standard Raku bisque kiln described above.) Occasionally pots bisqued in a gas or electric kiln are overfired. If this overfiring has proceeded to the extent of the body becoming dense the pots must not be glaze fired Raku style.

Carbon shadow decoration

One of the most beautiful decorative effects used in traditional red Raku is known as 'carbon shadow decoration'.

This decoration was first achieved by accident but later it was deliberately incorporated into the range of conscious decorative processes. Wares that touched one another during the bisque fire in the old style kilns tended to trap free carbon from the kiln atmosphere at the point of contact. This carbon was taken up by the clay surface and remained after cooling as a carbon 'stain'. The transparent or semi-transparent glazes of the red Raku style were applied to the bisque wares over the carbon stains which would remain trapped beneath during the glaze firing to eventually show through the glaze as grey, grey-brown or black 'shadows'.

Carbon shadow decoration is today achieved by three methods:

Charcoal and fireclay box method
This method is the one most commonly used in Japan and involves the use of a fireclay box or trough. The box is made from five flat slabs which are wired together during use. The two long sides of the box extend downwards beyond the level of the box's much perforated base to form a tunnel. Metal bars pass through holes in the side slabs and support the base slab (fig. 14).

When the Raku bisque kiln is unpacked those pieces for carbon shadow decoration are transferred to the fireclay box, into which they are placed mouth downwards and still warm. The fireclay box has been heated previously by a fire lit beneath it and when all the pots are in place the temperature is raised by thrusting briskly burning split timber into the tunnel beneath the box, until the box and its contents are hot. Broken pieces of charcoal are now dropped into the box between the pots where they ignite and impregnate the surface of the forms with which they are in contact with a random pattern of carbon stains.

The development of these carbon stains has to be watched carefully and as pieces appear to have reached a satisfactory state of carbonization they must be removed from the trough with tongs and quenched by dipping in hot water. This serves to 'freeze' the carbon pattern to the form. (Pots should not be left to soak in water at this stage. A brief dipping is quite sufficient to stabilize the carbon film.)

Standard kiln method
This method has the advantage of being achieved within the kiln chamber itself and therefore without recourse to the separate fireclay box.

The wares are bisque fired as normal in the standard bisqueing kiln. When the required bisque temperature has been reached the kiln lid is removed and the air supply holes at the base of the kiln are closed with mud. The temperature of the kiln will now slowly drop. Cooling should be allowed to proceed for about half an hour in this way, after which the lid may be removed from the saggar with a lid hook or with tongs. Broken pieces of charcoal and wood chips are then dropped directly into the saggar between the wares, where they will ignite and deposit carbon. The wares may now be removed from the saggar with tongs and quenched in hot water.

Electric kiln method
Since it is normally impractical or undesirable to burn materials directly within the firing chamber of electric kilns, the fireclay box method is used to deposit carbon shadows, after electric kiln bisqueing. However, a quick alternative is to remove the wares from the kiln with tongs as soon as they have reached the

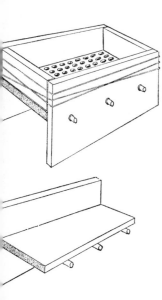

fig.14
fireclay box used for carbon shadow decoration

bisqueing temperature and place them in a metal receptacle containing small pieces of chopped wood or broken twigs or tree branches. The heat from the pot itself ignites the wood and carbon stains are deposited. The wares require only a few moments burning to be satisfactorily stained, after which they should be quenched in hot water.

8 Glazes for Raku

Glaze is a special category of glass which is fused onto the surface of the majority of pottery wares at high temperature in a kiln. In the case of Raku the glazes are traditionally of a lead boro-silicate composition, although lead silicate and other simple types are also suitable.

Glaze is applied to the bisqued pot as a calculated composition of inorganic earth minerals and chemicals suspended in water. The water from this fluid glaze is removed through absorption by the porous bisque ware body, causing a layer of the suspended particles to be deposited on the surface of the piece. When fired to the requisite temperature the minerals first sinter (see page 101) and then melt and fuse together to become liquid glass which, upon cooling, hardens into a glaze.

Most natural substances can be interchanged between the physical states of solid, liquid and gas by increasing or decreasing the temperature. As they cool from the liquid to the solid state, the vast majority of earth minerals take on a regular structure, known as the crystalline form. Most substances have distinctive crystalline forms which arrange themselves in an orderly modular structure. The form of the mass therefore, by extension, reflects the form of the individual crystalline form. This stable crystalline structure is suspended while any substance is in a liquid (or gaseous) state but re-forms upon cooling.

Glazes are atypical in that, although they may have been composed from materials having definite crystalline structures in their natural state, these structures are not re-established as the glass cools. Glass, and therefore glaze, rather than having the qualities of a crystalline solid, has the characteristics, including the visual appearance, of a liquid which has solidified but otherwise retained the qualities of its liquid state.

Zen, of course, is committed to the 'process of becoming' as the only meaningful condition of life, the concept of 'a final end product' or 'a completed process' being out of tune with reality. The arts of Zen, therefore, do not offer what the Western world would generally consider to be completed statements. Rather, they emphasize the vigour of the creative process, which is suddenly frozen in mid-stride so that the momentum in the work may be picked up, re-created and continued within the perception of the observer. The clear parallel between this attitude in art and the nature of glaze explains much of the popularity of ceramic wares in Zen circles.

Glaze types

Traditional black and red modes of Raku make use of two distinctive categories of glaze just as they use two separate clay bodies.

The higher fired black glaze is known in Japan as *kamoguro* because it is primarily derived from a dense iron and manganese-bearing rock dredged out from Kyoto's Kamo river and called *kamogawa-ishi*. Finely ground *kamogawa-ishi* is mixed with varied amounts of a ground glass material (technically a lead boro-silicate frit, see page 45) into some twelve glazes, each of which, due to a slightly increased percentage of the low temperature frit, is fractionally more fusible than its predecessor in the line. The *kuro* bowls are glazed with complex partial overpaintings of these glazes, starting with the most refractory and working towards the most fusible. By building up overlays of the more refractory glazes on certain areas of the bowl these may eventually be rendered dry and coarse in touch and appearance, with the glaze often little more mature than a sintered condition. Overpaintings of the softer glazes over the more refractory will produce the varied thick-bodied glazes with soft damp-looking surfaces typical of black Raku, while areas of the bowl built up only of the softer grades of glaze will melt to a fluid state and run down the sides of the bowl into the glaze welts known as *maku gusuri* (hanging fabric glaze) or *nagare* (tear drop glaze). The *kamoguro* firing range is 1200–1300°C.

Because of the difficulty in obtaining *kamogawa-ishi*, which is indispensable to true *kamoguro* glaze, potters outside Japan normally restrict themselves to glazes of the red Raku type. It is, however, possible for advanced Rakuists to develop simulated black style glazes which, while lacking some of the more subtle characteristics of the original, do react in an authentic manner. Even the red Raku style glazes can be modified within the general principle of the black glazes to produce a much more subtle and disciplined effect. Red Raku glazes are designed to mature between 750–1000°C.

Fluxes

The foundations of all glasses and glazes are built upon silica (SiO_2). When heated to 1710 °C silica melts to form a durable and resistant translucent glass. Such a high temperature is impractical for pottery purposes and it is reduced to more appropriate levels by means of substances known as fluxes. These fluxes are mixed with the glass-forming and other elements in the glaze composition and when fired together lower the overall temperature at which glass is formed. In red Raku glazes a combination of two very powerful fluxes, lead and borax, is used together to reduce the fusion point to the very low levels achieved in Raku kilns. The use of a combination of fluxes is more effective in lowering firing temperatures than a single flux alone.

Borax ($Na_2B_4O_7.10H_2O$)
Borax has the disadvantage of being a soluble flux; it is therefore best added to a glaze in the form of a frit. Borax loses its water of crystallization in a series of stages up to 318 °C, at which temperature anhydrous borax (sodium tetraborate $Na_2B_4O_7$) is formed. This substance melts at 741 °C and has improved resistance to solubility in very cold water.

Besides assisting in the melting of Raku glazes the boron content in the glass provides the most crucial visual characteristics of red style Raku glazes. It softens the excessive brilliance associated with glazes that use lead alone as a flux and thus satisfies the Raku requirement that it shall be 'soft and moderate in all things'.

Secondly, the boron imparts a slight quality of milky and opalescent semi-opacity. This tends to cloud the glaze, helping to mask the carbon shadows and underglaze work, removing them from the category of the transparently obvious and rendering the overall effect similar to that veiled and contemplative mood achieved in Southern Sung Ch'an Buddhist paintings, in which forms which emerge out of air and atmosphere itself are no less positive than mountains.

Glazes with a high lead content are commonly used for Raku and, while they are very satisfactory in themselves as glazes, they do require a boron content if they are to have those qualities that are fundamental to red Raku style glazes.

Lead compounds

There are a number of compounds of lead which may be used to provide the main fluxing agent in Raku glazes. These are: (1) white lead (lead carbonate, $2PbCo_3.Pb(OH)_2$), the most commonly used form; (2) red lead (Pb_3O_4), which is cheaper than white lead but, since it stains hands, wood and fabrics badly, is generally only used in making lead frits; (3) galena (lead sulphide PbS) and (4) litharge (lead monoxide PbO).

All these substances are toxic and great care must always be taken in their use. It is particularly important when working with lead in dry powdered forms that care is taken not to breathe it into the lungs. Wet glazes containing lead oxides should not be mixed with bare hands if there are any cuts or abrasions on the skin. All utensils should be thoroughly washed after use. Lead oxides should be kept in a locked cupboard, safe from children and those inexperienced in their use. In England the oxides of lead may not be used in schools (see appendix, 'lead poisoning').

Despite their toxicity, however, lead oxides are almost indispensable as fluxes in low temperature glazes. Besides the toxic forms, lead may be introduced into a glaze in a safe non-poisonous form known as a 'frit'.

Frits

Frits are combinations of materials which for convenience (such as protection against a poisonous constituent such as lead or, as in the case of borax, to render a soluble material into a form which is insoluble in water) have been melted together to form a stable compound in which such characteristics as toxicity and solubility have been eliminated at the same time retaining the necessary chemical properties of the constituents within the compound formed. This frit is ground down to a fine powder in a ball-mill for addition to glazes.

The most popular lead frits are made from lead and silica alone.
1 Lead monosilicate contains between 79 and 85 per cent lead and fires at approximately 750 °C,
2 Lead bisilicate (approximately 65 per cent lead) fires at approximately 900 °C,
3 Lead sequisilicate (approximately 68 per cent lead) fires at approximately 880 °C.
The three examples given above are standard lead silicate frits and are obtainable from most ceramic suppliers, who may well be able to offer other combinations as well as frits which contain, in addition to lead and silica, other desirable ingredients such as borax. Such low temperature frits may be used as the basis for a wide range of Raku glazes.

Both traditional black and red Raku glazes introduce their boron and part of their lead and silica content in the form of a Japanese frit known as *shiratama*. The frit as used by Nonko, Raku III (and handed on by him to his descendants as well as to Hon'ami Koetsu and Ogata Kenzan), is formed by melting borax, red lead and quartz together in a crucible. When the mixture is totally liquefied it is poured into a wet stone trough (or on to a wet concrete floor) and quenched with water. The glass shatters as it cools and may be reduced to a powder of suitable particle size in a ball-mill.

Composition: Quartz   38–39 per cent
             Red lead   50 per cent
             Borax   11–12 per cent

Shiratama frit may be used as a source of borax in many personal Raku glaze experiments. If you do not have the facilities to produce such a frit the nearest possible commercially produced frit may be substituted.

Basic red Raku glaze

A range of reds from salmon (*aka*) to scarlet (*shu*) is possible.

Aka

This colour can be obtained by including Japanese ochre in the clay body and/or by basting the green ware body with thick coats of ochre mixed with water.

The glaze used for red Raku is largely transparent and colourless and, although it modifies the colour somewhat as well as masking it behind the cloudy borax bearing glaze, it does allow the red body to show through.

Shu

The richer reds, such as the scarlet *shu* glaze devised by Nonko and extensively used by his successor Ichinyu, were the product of copper impurities in the silica used in this glaze, which were rendered a red colour in the reducing atmosphere of the kiln, thus making a more extreme modification of the body colour.

The guideline for the composition of the basic glaze, which is open to considerable personal variation, is as follows:

    Quartz sand, quartz or flint   20 per cent
    Shiratama (or substitute)   20 per cent
    Lead carbonate   60 per cent

Most Raku glazes have a tendency to peel off from the surface of the piece during the glaze firing; this is particularly prevalent in glazes which contain little or no clay. This problem is solved by the inclusion of a large measure of gum or siccative in the glaze mix. This burns away during firing but is nevertheless instrumental in strengthening the bond between unfired glaze and pot; it prevents both the tearing-off and peeling of an area of glaze by the tongs when the piece is set in the kiln.

The Japanese derive an effective siccative known as *funori* from a variety of seaweed boiled in water. Western substitutes include gum tragacanth, gum arabic, colloidal magnesium-aluminum-silicate, common size or starch. If glaze is kept in large batches the gum should be added only to the smaller amounts for immediate use, since some rapidly decompose and spoil the glaze. (A few drops of carbolic acid helps to delay this process.)

Typical glaze composition

Raku glazes are comparatively simple in nature and after a little practical experience most students can experiment and produce satisfactory personal glazes. The most essential requirement is to pay infinite attention to every stage of the process and to keep a detailed notebook of glaze composition, application and firing, since nothing is quite so frustrating as achieving a particular quality only to find that one has forgotten how it was done.

Raku glazes will be found to be primarily compounded from a comparatively short and recurring list of materials, but within which numerous variations are possible. It is advisable and certainly most instructive to work with only a limited number of glazes until you have thoroughly explored their possibilities and potentialities through modifying the constituents, varying the lengths of firing time, kiln atmosphere and post-firing treatments.

Typical compositional guidelines: temperature range 750–1000°C

	Percentage
Calcium borate frit[1]	75
Soda feldspar	15
Lead sequisilicate[2]	10
Gum[3]	

Calcium borate frit[1]	80
Soda feldspar	20
Gum[3]	

Calcium borate frit[1]	50
China clay	25
Quartz[4]	10
Shiratama[5]	15
Gum[3]	

Calcium borate frit[1]	60
Plastic vitrox (see page 111)	20
Shiratama[5]	20
Gum[3]	

	Percentage
Calcium borate frit[1]	50
Anhydrous borax	35
Lead sequisilicate[2]	15
Gum[3]	

*Lead carbonate	72
Quartz[4]	28
Gum[3]	

*Lithium carbonate	10
Lead carbonate	65
Quartz[4]	20
China clay	5
Gum[3]	

**Kuro Raku substitute*[6]

Lead carbonate	70
Quartz[4]	25
Shiratama[5]	5
Gum[3]	
+(for lower layers of glaze)	
Red iron oxide (Fe_2O_3)	8
Manganese dioxide (MnO_2)	3
Cobalt oxide (Co_3O_4)	2
(for upper layers of glaze)	
Red iron oxide (Fe_2O_3)	8
Manganese dioxide (MnO_2)	3

Fire very slowly

**Broken orange glaze*

Lead carbonate	72
Quartz[4]	18
Soda ash	2
Potassium bichromate	5
China clay	3
Gum[3]	

**Kuro Raku substitute*[6]

Lead carbonate	71
Quartz[4]	26
Anhydrous borax	3
Gum[3]	
+Fe_2O_3	9
MnO_2	4

Mix with a minimum of very cold water and use immediately.

**Kuro Raku substitute*[6]

Lead carbonate	52
Quartz[4]	33
China clay	10
Shiratama[5]	5
Gum[3]	
+Fe_2O_3	9
MnO_2	4

	Percentage		Percentage
*Bernard Leach Raku glaze base		Paul Soldner – semi-matt	
Lead carbonate	66	Gerstley borate	50
China clay	4	Kaolin	33·3
Flint[4]	30	Silica[4]	16·7
*Red glaze		*Potash feldspar	25
Lead carbonate	79	Colemanite	65
Soda feldspar	10	Lead carbonate	10
Quartz[4]	4		
Chromic oxide	4	Paul Soldner glaze	
Barium carbonate	3	Borax	50
		Colemanite	50
Paul Soldner – transparent base			
Gerstley borate	80		
Feldspar	20		

---

* Toxic glaze base.

[1] Colemanite may be substituted for calcium-borate frit as it has similar properties and is a source of boric oxide.

[2] Lead carbonate may be substituted, but the non-toxic fritted lead silicate is suggested here. Lead sequisilicate, comprising 68 per cent lead, has a firing temperature of about 880 °C.

[3] Amount: use as required.

[4] The forms of silica commonly used in glaze formulation (i.e quartz and flint) are interchangeable.

[5] If facilities for producing the shiratama frit are not available any low temperature lead boro-silicate frit may be substituted. Should neither of these be available, lead sequisilicate may be substituted in any glaze already containing a source of boric oxide.

[6] In order to achieve a range of firing variations within these glazes, such as exist in traditional black Raku, increase the proportion of flux to silica content.

Colouring glazes

The majority of glaze bases are, by themselves, colourless. These may be converted into coloured glazes by adding small amounts of metallic oxides or glaze stains, which are mixed into the glaze base. Some suggestions for colourant additions are given below. These figures represent percentages of the dry weight of the glaze base. The oxides may be added to the glaze while dry or thoroughly mixed into the liquid glaze slip.

	percentage		
Blue	0·5–0·75	cobalt carbonate	
	1	red iron oxide	
Turquoise	0·5	cobalt carbonate	(reduce strongly)
	1	chromic oxide	
White	5	tin oxide	
Grey	1–2	nickel oxide	
	or		
	2	iron chromate	(oxidize)

	Percentage		
Yellow	4–6	vanadium stain	
	or		
	4–6	tin-vanadium stain	
Brown	5	red iron oxide	
Green	3	copper carbonate	
	1	iron oxide	
Olive	5	iron chromate	(reduce strongly)
Bright red	3–5	cadmium selenium stain	
Copper red	1	copper oxide	(reduce strongly)
Burnt iron red	9	red iron oxide	(reduce strongly)
Black	8	red iron oxide	
	3	manganese dioxide	
	1	cobalt oxide	
Purple	5	manganese carbonate	(oxidize)
Tan	2	iron oxide	
Brown speckle	1	granular ilmenite	

Lustres

Small areas of metallic lustre are often produced on Raku wares by the conditions of heavy local reduction that take place during the secondary firing.

More controlled lustre may be produced by painting over the glaze a mixture consisting of one part of metallic sulphate, nitrate or carbonate with three parts of calcium ochre ground together in gum. The ware must be strongly reduced during firing and often needs to be burnished after cooling to reveal the full lustre effect. The best effects are obtained over the glazes of lower lead content.

Preparation of the fluid glaze from dry materials

Glaze preparation is a simple process, yet it must be carried out carefully and thoroughly. There are a number of points at which corners may be cut in order to save time and trouble; these almost never justify themselves.

Study the glaze recipe you plan to compose and check that all the constituents are available before you start weighing. If certain materials are not to hand substitutes are sometimes possible.

Make certain that you understand how the glaze recipe is given. The two common ways of rendering relative amounts of the constituents are as a percentage or as a simple proportion, e.g.

	Proportion	*Percentage*
Calcium borate frit	10	50
Anhydrous borax	7	35
Lead sequisilicate	3	15

Proportion recipes can be easily converted into a percentage if required. It is always preferable to convert your recipe to a percentage if you are contemplating controlled colourant additions and to compound your glaze in multiples of 100 g. units.

The first decision to be made concerns the amount of glaze you want to make. If you are planning only to conduct tests on a glaze 100 g. dry weight is mathematically convenient and is sufficient for three or four small tests to be conducted under different conditions.

1 Black Raku bowl

2 Interior of black Raku bowl showing the *Cha-damari* spiral

3 Undersides of Raku bowls showing foot ring designs

4 The Raku stamp: identification mark of Nonko

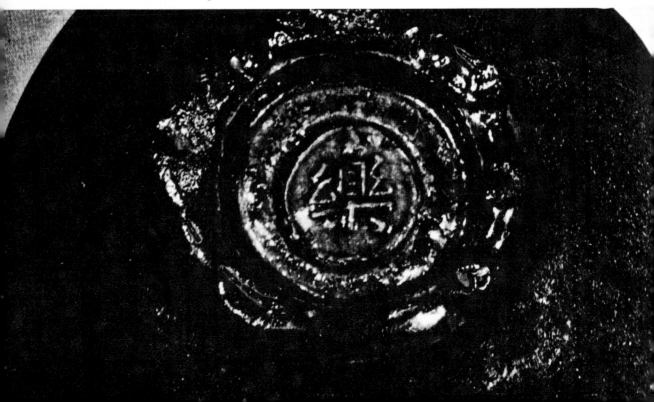

5 Entrance to a Tea House, Nara, Japan

6 Winter mode Raku *chawan* in the traditional style

7 Interior of a Tea House, Kyoto

9 Typical collection of personal tools suitable for making Raku wares

10 Wedging grog into a basic clay mass

11 Cross-section through a typical Raku clay

opposite
Wedging clay
13a Stage 1: *Aramomi* (press wedging)
13b Stage 2: *Nejimomi* (screw wedging)

12 Clay modification: layers of the basic clay are interspersed with layers of necessary additions before being wedged together

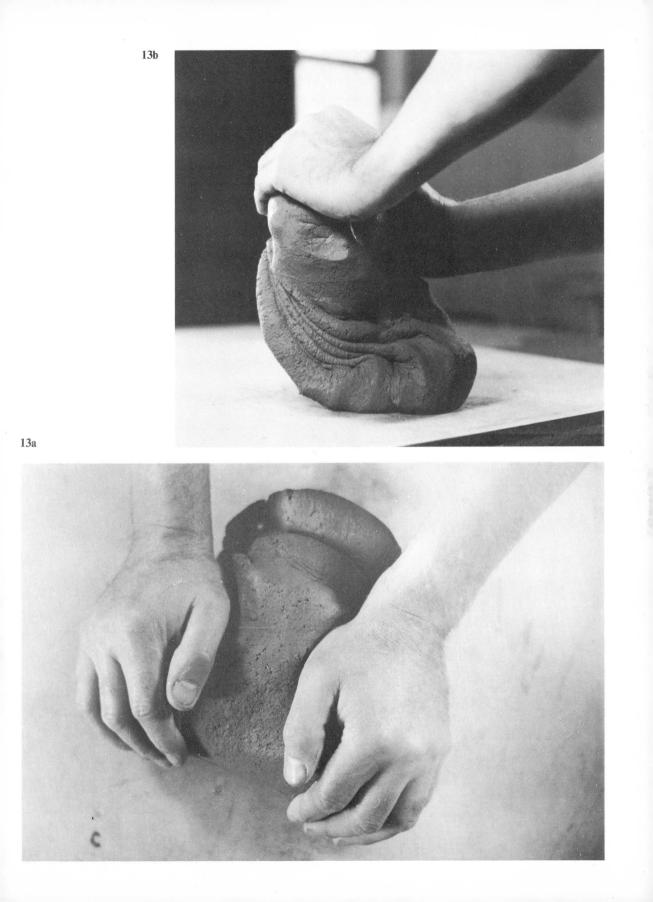

13b

13a

14 Clay modification by wedging in additional materials: the marbled pattern illustrated here
is typical of an insufficiently combined mixture; the clays must be wedged together until homogeneous

15 The forms, textures and colours of natural objects provide a constant source of reference
and stimulus

16 Part finished Raku bowl with a selection of tools suitable for carving

17 Using a surform tool to carve the walls of a Raku bowl

opposite
19 Painting underglaze decoration on to a thrown Raku bowl with a *fude* brush

20 Unglazed red Raku bowls showing carbon shadow decoration

18 Typical appearance of a bisque-fired Raku bowl

19
20

21
22

opposite
21 Painting overlays of glaze on to a winter mode Tea bowl with a *hake* brush

22 Glazing commercial red Raku bowls, Japan

23 Fitting a lid to a red Raku style saggar (a black style saggar is shown in the background)

opposite
25 Interior of a wood-burning red Raku kiln, Kyoto

26 Drying pots on a Raku kiln during firing

24 Building a coke-fired Raku kiln. The saggar can be seen in the main belly of the kiln and the paraffin flame gun, which will be used to effect a rapid initial rise in temperature, is directed into the air intake tunnel

25

26

27 Setting a Raku bowl into the saggar of a coke-burning kiln

28 Hooking out the saggar lid from a fuel-burning kiln

opposite
29 After the pot has been removed from the glaze kiln it may be given secondary reduction in
a container of combustible materials

31 Setting Raku pots into a small electric kiln

32 Firing non-traditional commercial Raku wares in an electric kiln, Japan

33 Raku brush pot glazed with several overlays of white and grey lead boro-silicate glazes and heavily reduced

34 Thrown Raku brush pot with black and silver-grey lead silicate glazes

35 Raku landscape sculpture incorporating carved and cast elements, glazed with heavily reduced white glazing, by Jill Crowley

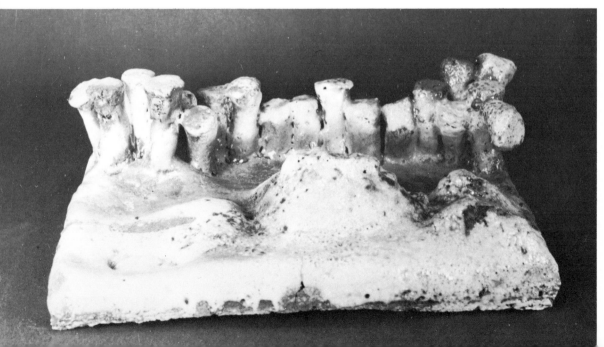

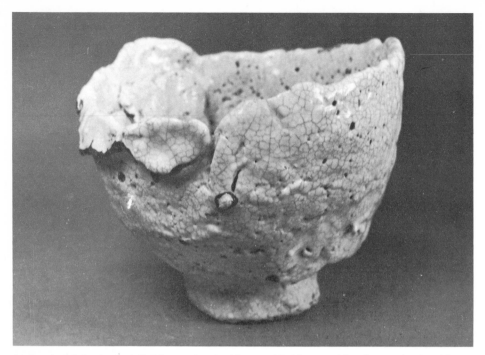

36 Bowl with freely modelled form, glazed with a crackled heavy white glaze and painted lustre decoration, by Jill Crowley

37 Carved Raku bowl, turquoise with painted lustre decoration, by Jill Crowley

38 Carved Raku vase, mottled tan glazes over a dark brown clay body

40 Thrown and torn Raku bowl, pale
salmon glaze contrasting with matt
black clay body

41 Raku bowl, glazed with grey and
white lead boro-silicate glazes

42 Carved Raku bowl, glazed with green and light tan lead boro-silicate glazes

43 Thrown Raku bowl, blue-green lithium based glaze

44 Carved bowl, heavily glazed with crazed off-white glaze, lip banded with fine silver, by
   Nancy Chernov

45 Low Tea bowl, glazed with eight layers of traditional Shiro style Raku glaze, decorated
   with overglaze iron brush work

46 Two thrown Raku boxes, glazed with lead silicate glazes and heavily reduced

47 Thrown Raku bottle form, black lead silicate glaze over blue and brown lithium glazes

48 Raku bottle, thrown, paddled and combed; glazed with blue, green and turquoise lithium glazes

49 *Maku* style Raku box, dark green glaze applied directly to green ware form

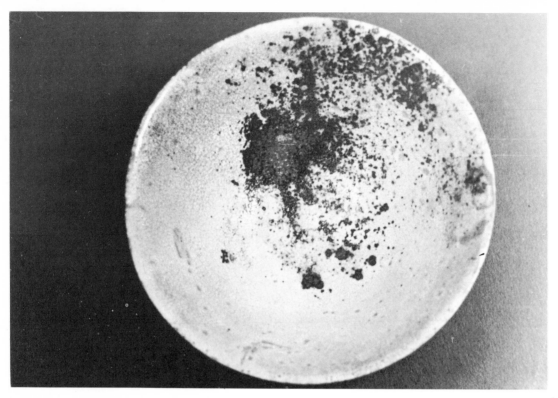

50 Interior of Raku bowl decorated with splashed oxide, by Nancy Chernov

51 Underside of the above bowl

Assuming that a glaze has proved satisfactory in tests and is to be used as a production glaze, batches of 500 g. or 1000 g. are more realistic amounts to compound. You quickly learn to relate the amount of any glaze to your needs for it.

Calculate the amount of each constituent glaze chemical required and check that these proposed amounts do, in fact, add up to the necessary total. (Many are the spoiled pots and defective glazes that can be traced back to faulty mathematics at this stage.)

An accurate set of scales capable of measuring weights down to fractions of one gram is essential for precise glaze compositions. Beam scales or beam balances are usually favoured by ceramists. Ensure that this apparatus is adjusted to indicate 'zero' when the chemical pan is empty.

As far as possible break up any lumps in the first constituent with the hands and pass a generous amount of it through a 40 mesh sieve. From this sieved material carefully weigh out the necessary amount according to the recipe. This process is repeated until each chemical has been weighed and individually sieved, when the ingredients may be put together into a large container. Any additions of metallic oxides or glaze stains are also weighed out and included at this time.

Mix the whole mass of dry materials by hand for a few minutes, after which a thorough dispersal must be achieved either by mechanical means such as a twin-shell blender or, more usually, by passing the superficially mixed chemicals through a 40 mesh sieve three times with hand stirring between each sieving.

Glazes composed of insoluble materials

Glazes composed of insoluble materials may now be mixed with water. Add an excess of cool water to the dry glaze chemicals in a clean non-porous container and mix the two together by hand until all lumps have been dispersed and the whole mixture is homogeneous. Cover the glaze and leave overnight. During this time the chemical particles will settle to the bottom of the container, leaving the excess of water on the surface. Siphon off this surface water, add gum solution to the glaze and thoroughly mix. A paint-mixing device powered by an electric drill is an excellent method of rapid homogenizing (fig. 15). Alternatively the glaze may be brushed through an 80 mesh sieve in addition to being mixed by hand (fig. 16). The glaze is now ready for use. It should be remembered, however, that the heavier particles in glazes settle quite quickly and consequently the glaze should be stirred at frequent intervals during use.

Fig. 15
An electric drill fitted with a paint-mixing attachment provides a rapid and efficient method of preparing glaze slips

Fig. 16
All glazes should be brushed through a sieve just before application: this disperses lumps in the glaze and assists in creating an even dispersal of the chemical constituents

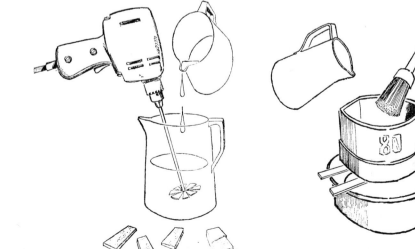

Glazes containing soluble materials

Materials that are soluble in their natural state are best introduced into the glaze as part of a frit. However, on occasions Raku glazes necessarily contain soluble chemicals in which case the glaze is best mixed and stored in the dry state and only mixed with water before use.

Start with only as much of the dry glaze compound as is required for immediate use, add the liquid gum and just sufficient cold water to make a mixture the consistency of cream. The glaze should be thoroughly mixed and applied to the ware as quickly as possible.

Aesthetic hazards in Raku glazing

A vast gulf seems to exist between the quality of the Raku style wares produced by the Raku potters in Japan and those produced elsewhere. The gulf is much wider, for example, than that which exists between potters making wheel thrown forms or enamelled wares. Part of the reason, of course, may be easily accounted for by the fact that the Japanese artists have behind them four hundred years of Raku experience and that their wares are the product of an exquisitely developed 'Tea' sensibility. But this still fails to explain why its Western counterpart is generally so poor; after all it too is born of 'sensibility' developed over a long cultural tradition and, while it may not be of the 'Tea' variety, it should nevertheless produce 'quality' within its own terms. It seems to be a fact that Western makers of Raku are not only prepared, but happy, to just go on producing very poor work – and one wonders how their sensibility can allow this to happen.

The reasons are perhaps not so difficult to isolate. In the West the 'immediacy' and the 'freedom' of the Raku self-development experience are its great attraction. This is also so in Japan, but there the 'immediacy' springs from Zen foundations and refers to an essence distilled from highest perceptions, while the freedom referred to is the freedom that intensive self-study and self-discipline allow the creative act.

One can forgive those new to Raku for being carried away by the intrinsic high level of excitement in the process, but once it has been experienced a few times the product has in itself to achieve a quality in proportion to the height of the Raku experience.

It must be emphasized that no element in Raku should outweigh any other and this includes the balance between the experience of the maker and the quality of the product. The failure of this principle of balance between the elements of Raku accounts also for another weakness in Western examples. Western makers see the glazing and glaze firing of Raku as its exciting and culminating focus; it is the 'high point' in the process. Yet in truth this is the antithesis of the Raku ideal. In Zen there are no 'good days' or 'bad days', neither has a routine or mundane task less potential for self-discovery than an exciting one. The lens of Zen is not so foolish as to make arbitrary points of focus. Yet so often students and potters spend hours compounding intricate and sophisticated glazes, applying them to their forms in a rich variety of ways and inventing many exciting ways to enrich the firing, secondary reduction and quenching processes – while the pot upon which this time and effort is lavished has itself been crudely formed in a couple of minutes.

If unsophisticated brevity is the characteristic of any stage in the Raku process then it must be the keynote to them all. But if the glazing and firing are to be involved and highly controlled then the form itself must have exactly parallel qualities.

This in some measure accounts for Raku being at one and the same time both the easiest and most difficult of the ceramic arts.

Glaze application

The range of possibilities that exists within the boundaries of the Raku glazing technique is as wide as your ability to explore it creatively. Every mood, colour, state of mind, texture, timbre, tone and density, from dramatic contrast through to the subtlest nuance, is possible. Which glaze to use and how it shall be used are the two problems which have to be considered and resolved. In pursuit of these there are three criteria of which you should be constantly aware; they are the criteria of suitability, honesty and directness.

There will be many possible ways of glazing any Raku form. Before you commit yourself to any one in particular take the time to assess in detail the character of the form itself. Since it is already an extension of yourself, a product of your own sensibilities and an index of your sensitiveness this is often deemed unnecessary and is neglected. But a pot is like a child: the fact that it springs from you does not justify your making it a vehicle for your own arbitrary whims, for it is also an independent entity to be treated with love and whose needs must be respected.

The glaze in your hands has the ability to violate, enhance, destroy, reveal, overwhelm, mask, compliment, devalue or debase the form. Which of these it does will depend upon the choices you make as to suitability of colour, thickness, fluidity, opacity and texture of the glaze. It will also be affected by how much of the surface of the form you choose to cover with glaze and how those glazed areas relate to those left bare. Furthermore, it will depend very much on the impression that is conveyed by the means you use to apply the glaze. A considered decision is necessary to all these problems so that your solutions may combine to create the most suitable possible relationship with the form and reveal its essential personality. You will quickly discover that scrupulous honesty to yourself and your tools and materials is indispensable. The way that glaze drips from a stick, streams from a slip trailer, pours from a jug or flows from a loaded brush are all totally distinctive and establish a particular glazing character. Try to discover the essential character of each and be discriminating in its use. Do not compromise your artistic principles by resorting to mere mannerisms (treat every pot as the individual it is) or the short-sighted dishonesty of trying to paint on the sort of glaze effect that pouring or dipping would naturally give you. The brush in particular is a source of inexhaustible variety and can be used for such different purposes as building up broad areas of glaze or sweeping round a bowl in an exuberant decorative choreography. You will amost certainly find that you need to practise its use and experiment with the variety of marks it offers. The brush should be well loaded with glaze and handled with confidence.

Finally, when you have decided the style of glazing best suited to the form and chosen the tools that are naturally best equipped to provide it the time comes to steady your mind, identify with the task in hand and combine mind and hand to its realization in an uncompromising act of commitment.

The most popular methods of glazing are outlined below.

Splashed glaze

Splashing is a quick and simple way to apply glaze and can be very effective for Raku since it conveys feelings of spontaneity, action and natural occurrence. Splashing itself is a dramatic event with a tense and exacting relationship between the performance of the action and the mark produced. The resulting splash is independently highly involving for the observer by virtue of its inherent vitality from movement and impact, which forces may easily be re-created in the mind.

Although splashing is always in large measure unpredictable, its effects can be controlled in a number of ways. These must be learned at first hand by practising splashing from a variety of sources (such as a large brush, the hand, a cup, etc.) and by varying the amounts of glaze used, the violence of the movement itself and the direction and distance over which the splash travels.

Splashing as a glaze effect is easily overdone. One splash on a form is often dramatic and exciting whereas a larger number may appear merely mundane and indecisive.

The Zen concept of harmony can sometimes be achieved by exactly balancing opposing forces such as a single splash of glaze on a regular and controlled form – perhaps reminiscent of a single raindrop on a rounded stone.

Dripped and dribbled glaze

Glaze may be dripped or dribbled on to a form from a slip trailer or from a brush or stick. If the surface is held horizontally the glaze dries in the droplets or trails where it has fallen or, if the form is held vertically, the glaze will tend to run down the form before drying. Glaze applied in this way has many of the kinetic qualities of splashed glaze and is often a very sympathetic treatment for Raku.

Poured glaze

Pouring is a common method of glazing many types of ceramics. The glaze should be carefully prepared and poured from a jug or ladle large enough to contain sufficient glaze for the whole task without having to refill it halfway through the process.

The form should be briefly dipped in clean water so that all surfaces of the piece may be lightly quenched.

If the form is hollow, glaze the inside first. This is done either by filling the interior with glaze and emptying it back into the jug immediately or, alternatively, a smaller amount of glaze may be poured into the form and the whole interior glazed by swilling the contents around before emptying.

The easiest way to glaze the outside of the form is to grasp it firmly in one hand near the base and hold it in an inverted position over a bowl. The glaze may then be poured over the form from near the base, to flow down over the whole surface as the pot is gradually rotated to be brought into line with the glaze flow (fig. 17).

If a number of overlayed glazes are desired each should be applied as soon as the preceding glaze film has dried to a matt condition.

Dipping

If an even glaze film is required a combination of pouring and dipping may provide the most satisfactory result (fig. 18).

The inside of a hollow form is first glazed by pouring, as described above, after which the form is again firmly gripped near the base and in the upside-down position is pushed downwards into a container of glaze so that the liquid rises up the exterior walls of the form to the desired level.

Thicker glaze films may be obtained by a number of dippings in the same or different glazes.

Wax resist decoration may be applied between glaze layers if desired.

Painted glaze

Traditional Raku is always glazed with a brush and many of its typical glaze qualities are directly derived from the characteristics of the brush itself.

Fig. 17
Glazing a bowl with overlays
of poured glaze

ζ. 18
azing by the 'pouring' and
'dipping and pouring'
methods

Any type of brush may be used, although the Japanese *fude* and *hake* varieties are the most suitable. The dried grass *hakeme* brush is easy to make and excellent for simple Raku glazing as well as for its more normal use in slip decoration. A range of brush sizes is desirable but not essential, large brushes being more useful than small ones.

The form should be quenched in clean water (somewhat more extensively than for poured glaze) immediately before glaze painting is begun. If this is not done the brush will 'drag' on the surface of the form and will not deposit a satisfactory stroke of glaze. Also, the glaze film will crack and tend to become detached from the piece during firing. The inside of the form should be painted first. If a number of different glazes with a range of melting points is to be used on any particular piece the inside is glazed with the more fusible glazes only.

On the exterior of the form many overlays of glazes may be built up. You should wait only until the surface layer is sufficiently stiff to handle before making the next application.

Some Raku potters take the precaution of painting the whole form with a coat of gum after the final layer of glaze has been applied.

Maku gusuri and *nagare* styles of glazing depend on careful calculation of glaze fusion points and a controlled pattern of overlays of the softer glazes during painting. It is also essential that glazes of this type are fired slowly.

9 Raku kilns

Most students first experience Raku-style firing using a commercially produced kiln in a studio situation. Some find that Raku, once experienced, is so rich in potentialities for developing perceptions, knowledge and personality that it becomes their predominant creative preoccupation. For others it provides a counterbalance of aesthetic involvement to the impersonal processes associated with industrially oriented ceramics. To every potter, however, it offers a deeper insight into the workings of kilns and into the nature of the subtle spectrum of responses that glazes make to fire.

If a multiplicity of techniques tend to separate potters into factions the study of fire is common to all and finally resolves all differences. Raku exceeds all other ceramic techniques in offering a comprehensive empirical kiln study, the results of which are assessed and assimilated not through instruments but through two of the potter's primary faculties, vision and 'the feeling of rightness'.

Commercially produced kilns are, on the whole, less instructive than those designed and built for oneself. They do, however, offer much that would not in any case be forthcoming from the more normal Raku type kilns and should certainly be experienced.

Buying a kiln

Most commercially produced kilns owned by private individuals, schools, colleges or departments of art are fired by piped gas or electricity. Either of these fuels is suitable for firing Raku wares.

Gas kilns have the advantage of offering a choice of reducing or oxidizing atmospheres while electric kilns normally produce only an oxidizing environment for the wares during firing. However, since most Raku reduction is achieved outside the kiln after the glaze has melted, this is not a serious handicap and is more than offset by the convenience of electric power.

If, after considering the low financial outlay and considerable aesthetic advantages of building your own fuel burning kiln, you are still inclined to buy a commercially produced kiln for Raku firing the following factors should be considered:

1 There is comparatively little to choose between gas and electricity as a fuel; each has advantages and disadvantages.
   (a) An electric kiln of suitable size involves a smaller financial outlay than a gas kiln of similar capacity.
   (b) Small electric kilns often run from the regular mains supply and do not require special wiring, but check with the kiln supplier.
   (c) Installation costs for gas kilns are usually high.
   (d) Electric elements tend to deteriorate quite quickly in kilns used for Raku style firing.
   (e) Small electric kilns are transportable.
   (f) Gas kilns offer both oxidizing and reducing atmospheres – electric kilns oxidize only.
2 Ideally Raku kilns fired by gas or electricity should have a firing chamber in the shape of a cube and be approximately $12 \times 12 \times 12$ in.
3 The choice between a top-loading kiln with a hinged or sliding lid and a front-loading kiln with a swing door is more a matter of personal preference than

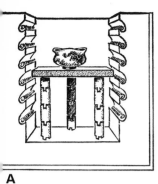

A

B

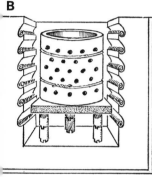

Fig. 19
Two methods (A and B) of
adapting top-loading kilns
for Raku glaze firing

Fig. 20
Modification of a large front-
loading kiln for Raku glaze
firing

practical advantage. Top-loading kilns are closer to the character of the traditional fuel-burning kilns and are consequently usually preferred. The only really important factor in either of these two types of kiln is that the door or lid can be opened and closed quickly and easily.

4 Electric kilns should be fitted with a switch which automatically cuts off the current when the kiln door is opened.

5 A thermoelectric device fitted to the kiln for indicating firing chamber temperature (such as a thermocouple and pyrometer) is useful but not essential since Raku glaze firing is visually gauged for maturity.

6 The kiln must have a spy-hole which allows visual observation of the wares being fired.

7 The ability of the kiln to effect very rapid rises in temperature is a positive advantage. Also, the possibility of cutting back the fuel supply so that existing temperatures can be simply maintained is very desirable.

Converting a kiln for Raku

It is possible to fire Raku glazes in almost all designs of commercially produced kilns.

Small kilns normally require no modification other than the protection of the firing chamber floor against the runny Raku glazes by a kiln shelf which has been thickly painted with several layers of bat wash (50 per cent kaolin, 50 per cent flint mixed with water to the consistency of thin cream).

Larger kilns may well prove to be uneconomic propositions for Raku but can nevertheless be satisfactorily used if desired. Normally the size of the firing chamber has to be reduced to a more practical size.

Two methods (A and B) of decreasing the chamber size of top-loading kilns are illustrated (fig. 19). Method A consists of simply reducing the effective depth of the chamber through the introduction of a kiln shelf set on castellated props to the level appropriate to the size of the wares to be fired. Method B also reduces the kiln depth but additionally employs a saggar as the firing chamber. This has the advantage of containing the fragments of any wares that should shatter during firing and thereby protecting the kiln.

Large scale front-loading kilns may be converted to fire Raku through the use of a box saggar set on a raised shelf within the kiln (so that the kiln peep-hole is still effective). The area of the kiln mouth surrounding the saggar may be filled with fire-bricks (fig. 20).

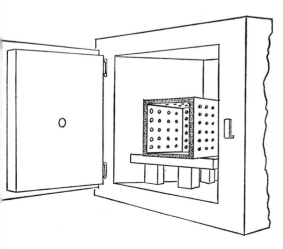

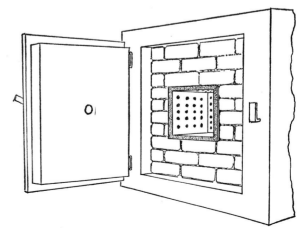

It is advisable to use for Raku only those electric kilns fitted with a device which automatically discontinues the current when the kiln door is opened. If such a device is not fitted the power to the kiln must be switched off before the kiln is opened.

When using gas kilns for Raku firing it is advisable to open the kiln dampers before opening the kiln chamber for the introduction or removal of wares.

Building a fuel-burning kiln

In common with most aspects of Raku, there are those kilns which traditionally have been used by the Raku family for the production of their wares and those modified designs that, because of the availability of certain fuels or for other practical reasons, are more suitable for our present needs. Even with modified designs the general principles of the traditional kilns are often respected and tend to underlie most modern variations. In any case a knowledge of the traditional kilns imparts indispensabie understanding to a vital part of the Raku process. It should be remembered that two of the keynotes of Zen and of Raku are self-reliance and self-knowledge and, however happy we may be with the Raku wares we achieve from commercially produced kilns, this is sure to be reduced with the knowledge that the work is not totally a product of our own understanding and sensibility until the whole process, including the kiln, has been designed and controlled for ourselves by ourselves.

Kilns are essentially pragmatic beings, each is individual and idiosyncratic. No hard and fast rules govern their design, only general principles. They have to be patiently and lovingly built, fired, understood, modified and cooperated with; only in this way are the subtleties of design and operation unfolded.

Traditional Japanese Raku kilns are of two types. These relate to the two classic categories of black and red wares. Black Raku is much the higher fired of the two and its forms are very rapidly glaze fired in a small charcoal-fuelled kiln whose high temperature is achieved by the use of a bellows system. Red Raku, on the other hand, has a glaze of lower maturing temperature and the wares are fired in small batches and at a slower rate. Both styles of kiln are designed to be opened and closed quickly for the removal of the red-hot wares. Variations on the black Raku firing technique are most commonly used by Western potters, although kiln designs for this process are as often based on the red Raku style kiln as upon the black.

Fig. 21
Method of carving a saggar lid from a wheel-thrown basic form

The general requirements for a Raku kiln may be summarized as below:
1 Small size.
2 Simple low-cost construction.
3 Fast firing on easily available, convenient and economical fuel.
4 High thermal efficiency per fuel unit.
5 A firing chamber that can be easily and quickly opened and closed with minimum loss of heat.
6 Good thermal insulation to avoid undue heat loss through kiln walls and to make it possible to work in close proximity to the kiln.
7 A means of observing the wares being fired.
8 A means of controlling temperature.
9 Rapid heat loss recovery time.
10 Easy to modify should the need arise.

In response to these requirements certain basic kiln concepts were devised by Chojiro (Raku I) and, although much modified by his descendants, have in principle remained to the present day.

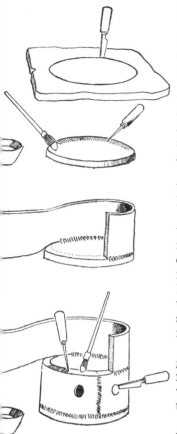

The firing chamber

The firing chamber consists of a lidded fireproof box known as a saggar. This is thrown (fig. 21), or made by coiling or slab building (fig. 22), either from a plastic fireclay and sand mixture or black Raku body or saggar clay (some sawdust may be included to increase the eventual ease of heat penetration).

Saggars range in size from about 8 to 15 in. diameter (fired size), depending upon the type of kiln and firing technique to be used. They are generally about one-third higher than they are wide and about $\frac{1}{2}$ in. thick. The walls of the saggar are penetrated with holes (fig. 23). For black Raku fired by charcoal these holes should be about the diameter of a pencil, but for other styles they can be as large as $1\frac{1}{2}$ in.

In order that a saggar may continue to be usable even after it has cracked (a very common occurrence) it is normally banded with heat resistant wire after it has been bisque fired.

The saggar lid should be domed in shape and surmounted by a large handle which allows it to be easily lifted free of the saggar body, or replaced, with a minimum of difficulty. The saggar lid should be made so that the handle is carved from the parent mass rather than be modelled on to it (fig. 21). The lid itself is usually penetrated with a hole about 1 in. in diameter which allows the Rakuist to observe the interior of bowl forms. This sight hole is sometimes fitted with a plug. As a precaution against the handle breaking from the saggar lid two small additional holes may be drilled through the lid. If necessary, a wire handle may be passed through these.

Visual access to the interior of the saggar is essential so that the progress of the glaze melt may be followed. This is most easily achieved by means of a steel or fireclay tube, one end of which passes through one of the holes in the saggar wall while the other passes through the outer wall of the kiln to provide a viewing tube.

An alternative means of viewing the interior of saggars used for firing Raku plates and dishes is achieved through a large central hole in the saggar lid, which is plugged when viewing is not taking place. A regular lid hook is used to remove the plug but a special set of tongs is required to lift the saggar lid.

fig. 22
forming a saggar by the slab-building method

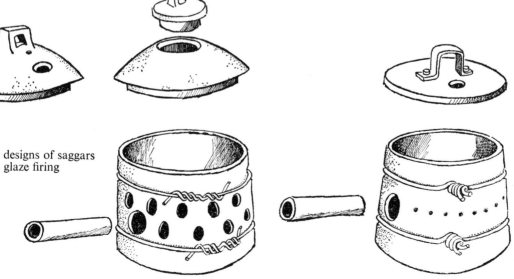

fig. 23
alternative designs of saggars for Raku glaze firing

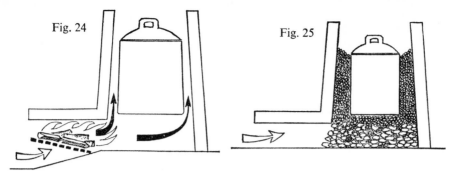

Fig. 24   Fig. 25

Firing method

There are two methods of applying heat to the saggar and several kiln variations are possible for each of the methods.

Type 1 An updraught of heat is directed through the kiln from fuel burning in an external firebox (fig. 24).

Type 2 Heat generated from fuel which is contained within the belly of the kiln itself, packed around the saggar (fig. 25).

Kilns that combine these two firing methods are also popular and tend to be very efficient.

Wood-burning kilns

Wood is the most common kiln fuel used by Japanese potters and the majority of the most famous Japanese wares are fired by means of it. A number of these wares, such as Bizen, Iga and Tamba, draw many of their particular qualities directly from some aspect of the character of wood as a fuel. The subtleties of kiln design for wood fire are well understood and it is therefore not surprising that many Raku kilns operated in Japan outside the Raku family tradition should be versions of the standard wood-burning design, adapted to meet Raku requirements.

Kiln efficiency is a more important factor in the updraught design than in the type 2 (fuel filled belly) kilns. Here poor design will cause excessive consumption of fuel with an insufficient concentration of heat where it is required. It is important that the heat is not allowed to pass through the kiln without making its maximum contribution to the temperature level.

Fig. 26
Simple wood-burning Raku kiln (type 1): the open conical cover (**B**), which is removed to allow access to the saggar, acts as a simple chimney. The primary air route into the kiln (**A**), passes through the hottest part of the fire

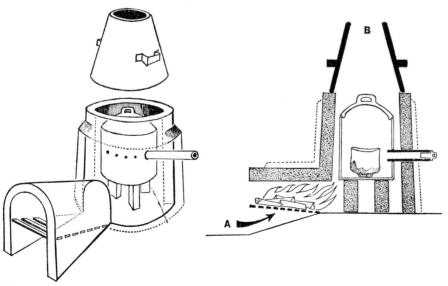

27
ditional style of small
wood-burning kiln adapted
to the needs of Raku (type
): the proportions of the
firebox can be seen at the
lower right of the diagram

The following design factors should be given attention:
1 The size of the grate must be related to the size of the kiln. The intensity of
heat obtained within the kiln chamber of an efficiently designed kiln is propor-
tional to its grate area.
2 Do not allow a clear gap beneath the fire bars as this allows comparatively
cool air to be drawn into the kiln. Ideally the bars slope downwards into the
kiln mouth so that all primary air drawn in has to pass through the fire. This
primary air intake should be larger than the fuel mouth.
3 The gap left between the saggar and the walls of the kiln must compromise
between being sufficiently wide to allow an efficient draught to operate and
narrow enough to extract the maximum play of heat on the saggar walls. A gap
of between 1 and 2 in. covers most variations in saggar size and kiln design.
4 Draught may be controlled through the size and shape of the kiln chimney. A
tapering chimney reduces atmospheric pressure and therefore increases the
draught. The approximate diameter of the chimney at its point of departure from
the kiln should be one-quarter of the diameter of the kiln belly at that same
height. For maximum effect the height of chimneys should exceed their diameter
by several times. In Raku kilns chimneys have the additional purpose of directing
smoke away from the potter's working position at the kiln mouth.
5 The area of heat inlet from the firebox should exceed the area of outlet to the
chimney.
6 The chimney should be constructed on a stable brickwork base. The kiln walls
may be made of a single thickness of firebricks or common red bricks (although
in this latter case it is desirable to use firebricks for the part of the fire mouth
nearest to the kiln body). The outside of the kiln should be covered with 2 to
3 in. of clay slurry mixed half-and-half with sand (mud and sand is a perfectly
acceptable substitute). This insulating material should be bonded together by the
inclusion of dry grass or cut straw and be applied in as dry a condition as

workability allows. The kiln should be given a preliminary firing to dry out the bricks and insulation as well as to test the heat flow before the actual Raku glaze firing.

7 The firebox mouth should be fitted with a simple damper to control the air intake to the kiln.

Fuel

Since a long flame as free of sulphur as possible is desirable for Raku firing light resinous wood, such as dry, split thin pine, is the best fuel. The average Raku kiln fired on this fuel reaches operating temperature in about three to four hours. (The use of some timber soaked in sump oil, as mentioned elsewhere, will assist in reducing this time.)

The timber is often lit in a separate fire before going into the kiln grate.

It is important to feed the wood into the kiln at the most efficient rate. Many potters inexperienced in wood-burning kilns tend to stifle the kiln through excessive fuel supply. The use of timber which has not been split into sufficiently small pieces is not advised.

Charcoal fired kilns

Charcoal is the only fuel suitable for firing the traditional *kamoguro* glazes and is the most attractive of all possible fuels.

Kilns fired with charcoal offer a rapid achievement of the heat necessary for firing as well as the ability to be sensitively controlled for subtle and minute variations of temperature. The latter attribute is essential for such effects as *maku gusuri* and *nagare*.

Unfortunately, the charcoal obtainable in the West seems to compare rather poorly with the long-burning Japanese variety. This tends to belie the efficiency of the Japanese originals and encourages experiment with other fuels.

Charcoal kilns depend upon a controllable supply of pressurized air which fans the fuel. Japanese kilns usually make use of a bellows system but an air compressor, an air pump or an old vacuum cleaner set to reverse, are perfectly workable substitutes.

The kiln is kindled with some previously ignited charcoal, to which unlit charcoal may be added; the air fanned fire ignites each addition of charcoal. Charcoal is added until the belly of the kiln is filled as far as the saggar lid. It is important to keep the charcoal well tamped down during firing.

Coke burning kilns

Coke is, in many ways, the best fuel to use as a substitute for charcoal in the type 2 (fuel filled belly) category of kiln. It has the advantages of being economical and efficient to use as well as being comparatively cheap and easy to obtain. Once operating temperature has been reached it can be maintained for a number of hours with only a minimum of attention to feeding, tamping and raking out.

Design A (fig. 29) illustrates a simple and efficient type of coke-burning kiln which can be built from about seventy common red bricks and three firebricks. It consists of a cylindrical wall of common bricks, assembled without mortar and tapering slightly as it rises in height.

The kiln is built around the saggar so as to leave a gap of about three inches between the top of the saggar and the kiln wall. The saggar itself is raised off the ground on the three firebricks placed as shown.

The kiln is fed with air through a tunnel vent at the front of the kiln. The vent itself has a horizontal partition (made from a broken kiln shelf) which extends into the belly of the kiln as far as the middle of the saggar. This prevents the air

Fig. 28
Variation on the design of the traditional black Raku kiln, making use of the normal combination of charcoal and forced air. The air is supplied through a tube (**A**); a number of closable ash removal ports (**B**) must be built into the foundation layer of the kiln. Charcoal kilns are capable of relatively high temperatures and must be built of firebrick throughout

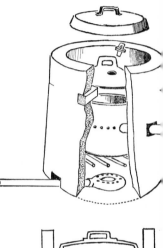

A

Fig. 29
Coke-burning kiln (design A)
incorporating a split level
air intake for efficient firing

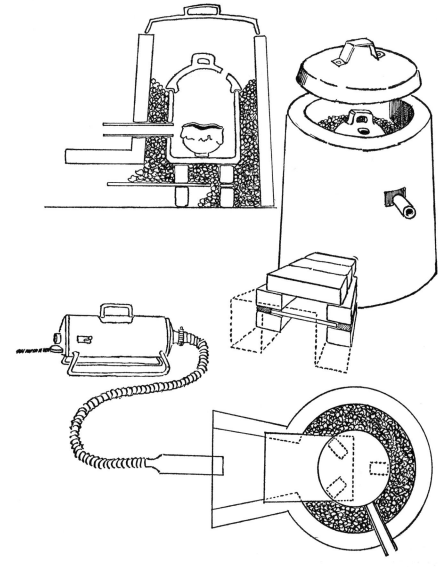

passage becoming choked with fuel and ensures an air supply to the back half of the kiln. This simple device prevents the formation of 'hot and cool spots' in the firing chamber.

The kiln should be lit with wood, coke being added slowly once a brisk fire is established. (If you have access to a paraffin flame gun, as described on page 95, it will provide a quick and efficient means of lighting and building up the initial working temperature in this kiln.)

Temperature may be controlled through the operation of a simple damper on the air supply vent and through additional air vent bricks on the foundation level of the kiln.

The effectiveness of this kiln is very greatly increased by having a supplementary forced air supply, such as can be provided by a compressor or a pump.

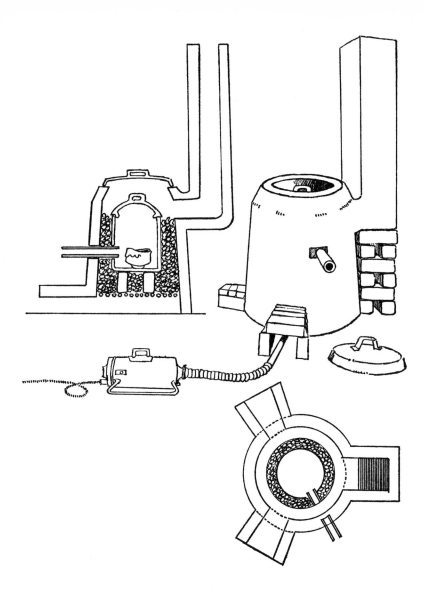

Fig. 30
Coke-burning kiln (design B)
incorporating twin air
intake ports and chimney;
a source of forced air
greatly increases the
efficiency of this kiln

Design B (fig. 30) is an improved, twin vent coke-burning kiln with a chimney. It is efficient and a particularly good design when a large firing chamber is required. It is built from about 110 common red bricks and three firebricks.

Design C (fig. 31) has four intake ports and a chimney.

Forge kilns

Forge kilns are the most common variety of indoor Raku kilns in the West and are a direct transcription of the traditional black Raku charcoal kiln to more common Western fuels.

Forge kilns are particularly suitable for the firing of bowls and test wares. These kilns tend to be small in size and remarkably efficient.

The kiln consists of a box built from standard firebricks, which contains a

Fig. 31
Coke-burning kiln (design C)
with four air intake ports
and a chimney; simple
dampers may be used to
control air intake

Fig. 32
Variations on the traditional
black Raku style forge
kilns. These are designed to
burn coke or solid
smokeless fuel. Forced air
is supplied to the kiln
through an inlet (**A**)

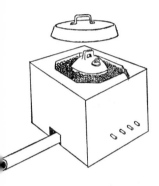

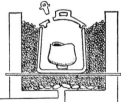

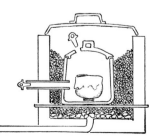

saggar packed around with coke (fig. 32). Saggars should be a little deeper than
for other varieties of kilns and small in diameter.

The kiln may be lit with a gas and air mixture (the gas being discontinued after
a good fire has been achieved) or with coke transferred from a fire. The forced
air quickly rejuvenates the fire and the kiln may be filled to its working level.

Forge kilns should only be used in conjunction with a room air extraction
system.

Kilns fired on a combination of coke and paraffin
The paraffin flame gun is an inexpensive source of high temperature forced fire
and is a highly desirable piece of supplementary equipment for any individual or
ceramics department contemplating Raku work.

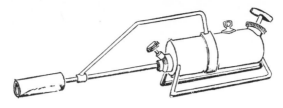
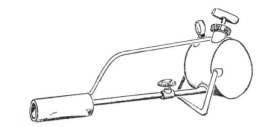

Fig. 33
Two common designs of the
paraffin flame gun

The flame gun mixes air with a vaporized jet of paraffin oil to produce a high velocity directional flame that is ideal for directing into the fire mouth or air vent of any type of kiln for quick ignition and rapid initial temperature rise.

Kilns designed specifically for the use of the flame gun as the primary heat source have the advantages of very small size and of being quick to achieve firing temperature. However, when the flame gun is used in conjunction with coke a sensitive temperature control with less heat loss during removal of wares from the kiln is achieved than is possible through the use of the flame gun alone.

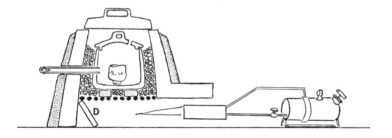

Fig. 34
Two small scale kilns, fired
  on coke supplemented with
  a paraffin flame gun,
  offering rapid and efficient
  firing. If the kilns are
  intended to be semi-
  permanent they should be
  built with refractory
  firebrick throughout. The
  flame deflector (D) is made
  from a piece of broken kiln
  shelf.

Fig. 35
Kiln designed for indoor or outdoor Raku firings. This kiln
can be fuelled either by a
mixture of gas and air or
alternatively with the
paraffin flame gun. A simple
brick structure (**A**) may be
designed to support the kiln
lid when it is slid open. The
rest of the kiln is built with
refractory firebricks; the lid
and firing platform are
made from kiln shelves

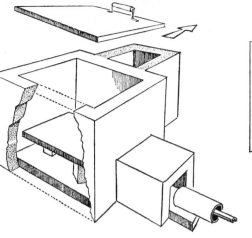
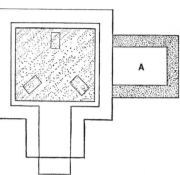

Fig. 36
Variation on the Japanese
portable kiln. This design
uses an oil drum as a shell
and is lined with refractory
brick; the firing platform
and flame deflector are
made from pieces of kiln
shelf. A mixture of air and
gas is used to fire this kiln
(the paraffin flame gun may
be used as an alternative
source of heat)

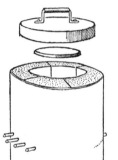
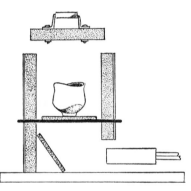

Fig. 37
Small scale Raku kiln for indoor
or outdoor use which may be
fired either with a mixture
of air and gas or with the
paraffin flame gun. The
kiln is built entirely from
refractory firebricks; the
roof support, firing
platform and flame
deflector (**D**) are pieces of
kiln shelf. The source of
fire must be discontinued
before this kiln is opened

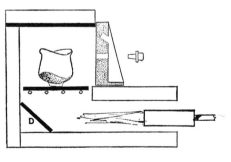
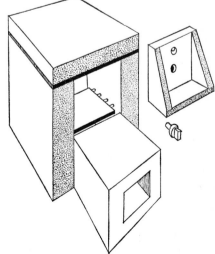

Kilns fired with paraffin or with a gas and air mixture

Kilns may be fired with the paraffin flame gun or with a mixture of forced air and gas. While the air and gas mixture may be used indoors or out, the paraffin flame gun should only be used out of doors. In the latter case the air and gas are pumped separately into a refractory tube in which they mix *en route* to the ignition point at the mouth of the kiln firebox. The gas flame should always be lit before the forced air supply is connected.

These kilns do not necessarily make use of a saggar. The wares can be placed directly on to firing platforms within the kiln, around which heat rises from below. The more or less direct play of the flame on the glaze surfaces tends to produce a variety of effects unlike those achieved in kilns employing saggars.

The forced flame should be discontinued during the packing and removal of wares from the chambers of these kilns.

Kilns fired by a combination of charcoal and wood

Traditional red Raku is fired in a kiln which combines the fuel filled belly design with the external firebox style. The kiln is loosely packed with charcoal around the saggar but, instead of being fanned with forced air as in the black Raku version, it is fed with an updraught of heat from a wood burning firebox (fig. 38).

The rise in temperature tends to be very slow in this type of kiln and temperature is controlled through the operation of the damper at the firebox mouth. Precise chimney design for a brisk draught is essential.

Unlike black Raku, which is placed directly into the hot kiln, red Raku is normally packed into the saggar when the kiln is well below firing temperature. The temperature of the wares is brought up to the maturation point of the glaze with the kiln. When glaze maturation has been reached the wares are removed with tongs, as for the black style, but are allowed to air cool slowly.

Red style kilns usually take about three hours to reach packing temperature.

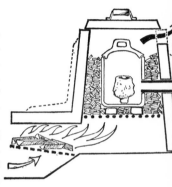

Fig. 38

10 Raku glaze firing

Newly built, fuel-burning Raku kilns benefit greatly from a light preliminary firing before the day on which the Raku glaze firing is to take place. As well as drying out the bricks and mud lagging which will otherwise slow down the early rise in temperature on glaze firing day, this will enable you to become acquainted with the firing characteristics of your kiln (and make modifications to its design if necessary). Since kilns are highly individual and idiosyncratic pieces of equipment you can expect to achieve better results from a kiln as you experience it and its firing characteristics.

A Raku kiln works most efficiently after several hours of firing, when all its components are thoroughly saturated with heat. Disappointing results are often obtained through impatient use of the kiln before it is really ready. All too often students are ready to end their day's work just as the kiln reaches peak performance, which can then be maintained almost indefinitely if tended.

The most effective temperature build-up to firing temperature occurs when a fully stoked kiln is adequately supplied with oxygen. It is important, therefore, to maintain a steady up-draught through the kiln with the dampers fully open. The dampers may be put into operation to either equalize or consolidate the kiln temperature as the firing temperature is approached.

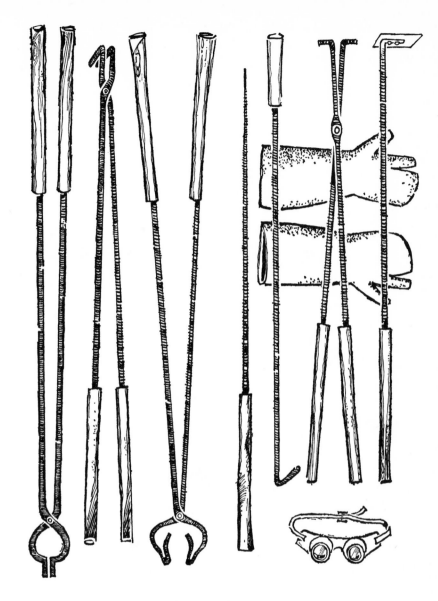

Fig. 39
Equipment for glaze firing: asbestos gloves and protective goggles together with a full set of firing irons (*from left to right*): tongs for use with top-loading kilns; two pairs of tongs for removal of wares from front-loading kiln; charcoal tamper; saggar-lid hook; tongs for removing alternative (handless) design of saggar lid; ash rake

It is usual to light and build up the temperature of the kiln from cold with a pot already in the saggar. This may be checked from time to time as the temperature rises, as the melting of its glaze is the indicator that the kiln has reached operating temperature. It is also usual to stand the pots to be glazed that day either on or near the kiln to remove any last vestiges of dampness.

Equipment necessary for glaze firing

1 Long-handled tongs. These should be light in weight and well balanced. The jaws must have a positive grasp and be set at the appropriate angle for removing wares from the particular design of kiln being used.
2 Lid hook, with which to remove lids of either kiln or saggar.
3 A pair of long asbestos gloves for the Rakuist (and if necessary for his firing

99

assistant), or long mittens made of several thicknesses of cloth or long strips of material which may be wound around the hands and arms. These may be dampened to help protect against the heat.

4 Shatter-proof goggles are an excellent safety precaution as well as protecting the eyes from the effects of smoke and fumes, which can often make vision difficult at exactly the point in time when it is most necessary. (The shatter-proof goggles fitted with shaded polarized glass which are widely available from military surplus stores also help to clarify vision when attempting to assess events within the incandescent kiln interior.)

5 A lidded metal container to hold combustible materials for the secondary reduction stage; also, an ample supply of these materials – dry leaves, sawdust, wood chips, etc.

6 A container of water for quenching and washing the fired wares.

If you have never glaze fired Raku before you can expect a new and exciting experience for, whereas most other types of pottery are fired 'blind' by some kind of instrumentation, in Raku glazing the reaction to fire is directly available to see and control. By watching the glazed pot through the kiln's viewing tube, spyhole or aperture one can observe the glaze sinter in its first stage of changing state and gradually liquefy and start to flow.

The glaze on certain parts of the form will melt before others; some parts, such as the insides of deeper thick forms, will be slow to fuse. (For this reason it is not advisable to use a viewing tube which is so small in diameter that you are able to observe only a tiny part of the glaze surface.) Thickness of pot and of glaze will be important factors in the glaze melt. As the result of the knowledge gained from these direct observations you will modify your future glaze compositions, combinations of glazes used together and methods of application.

Not only is it possible to watch the glaze melt – it is also possible to control and modify it. If, for example, the glaze on some parts of the piece is already starting to flow while in others it is still immature, the temperature rise of the kiln needs to be cut back so that a slow soak takes place: release a little heat from the kiln by briefly lifting its lid and then control the temperature through draught and dampers. A very slowly rising temperature with regular soaking to heat saturate the piece provides the best conditions for Raku firing.

The kiln atmosphere can be changed from oxidation to reduction or vice versa by controlling the rate of oxygen supply, thereby inducing distinctive colour changes. (Often the introduction of pieces of burning wood into the air supply tunnels before cutting off the oxygen supply with the dampers produces a more effective reduction in the kiln.)

Numerous other modifications during firing are possible and it is the discovery and use of these that provides one of the most exciting areas for experiment in Raku.

On most occasions it is preferable to glaze fire Raku pieces individually so that they can each receive individual attention. However, it is possible for several pieces to be set in the kiln at the same time if the saggar is sufficiently large to contain them. (Since the wares are removed while the glaze is still fluid it does not matter if the pieces touch one another while in the saggar.) Although several pieces may be set together they do not, of course, need to be removed all at the same time, and indeed it is quite unlikely that the ideal time for removal of all the pieces would occur simultaneously. Individual pieces may be removed when they are ready and new ones may be introduced in their place. If, as sometimes happens, you are working with a clay body that has been insufficiently tested or developed it is inadvisable to fire by the batch method, since if an occasional piece shatters in the kiln it may well also ruin a number of other wares that would otherwise fire without mishap.

It is often much easier to set a Raku form into a kiln than it is to remove it.

Consider this problem carefully before placing items in the saggar, since you may well require tongs of a different design to remove them, or possibly an unglazed Raku spur may have to be set in the kiln beneath the piece so that it can be readily retrieved. (This is particularly so of tile forms.)

During the melt the glaze will pass through five stages, each of which can be observed through the peep-hole:

Stage 1 The glaze darkens and burns out the gum it contains.

Stage 2 The change of state from solid to liquid is preceded by a condition known as sintering, in which the glaze film often cracks and takes on a coarse appearance; these characteristics gradually heal over as the glaze progresses towards the liquid state. This sintered stage is too early for the removal of the pot.

Stage 3 After sintering the glaze fuses together into a thick glutinous condition with a slight surface sheen. Provided that the kiln temperature has been controlled so that the glaze on all parts of the piece has reached this stage of maturation, now is an ideal point to withdraw the form from the kiln.

Stage 4 The surface sheen on the glaze increases and bubbles rise slowly through the glaze to form and eventually burst on the surface. Once these bubbles have started to form it is best to leave the pot in the kiln until they have all disappeared. If it is removed during this stage the glaze will cool with thin fragile layers of glaze over pockets of gas. These break easily leaving very sharp, dangerous edges.

If a pot is accidentally removed from the kiln before all the bubbles have dispersed it may be immediately returned to the kiln, provided that it has not been quenched in water.

An interesting pitted effect may be achieved by removing the form from the kiln while the bubbles are very active and allowing it to air cool. The many bubbles can now be broken with a light tool and the pot returned to the kiln for the sharp edges of the fractures to fuse over and become smooth. As soon as this has been achieved the pot is removed from the kiln and treated in the normal Raku manner.

Thick glaze, and particularly the *maku gusuri* effects, demand a very sensitive control of this stage of fluidity through temperature soaking.

Stage 5 The final stage of the melt is for the glaze to become extremely glossy and very fluid. It forms into pools of liquid glaze on horizontal surfaces and runs on vertical ones.

When cooled, glazes which have been allowed to reach this stage of melt have a hard, dense and very shiny surface, which is quite out of character with the soft modulated qualities traditionally associated with Raku but which may, however, relate well to certain other types of form.

The sensitivities and attention of the Rakuist have to be sharpened to the point where he experiences a complete and extended state of rapport with the form; a few moments of inattention at a critical point in the process may cause an irrecoverable loss of control and the whole concept of the piece may be lost.

Firing routine

The development of an efficient firing routine is essential in Raku if excessive heat loss, and long periods of temperature recovery, are not to occur on each occasion that a pot is either introduced into or removed from the kiln.

Raku glaze firing is an extremely precise and controlled process and demands a state of calm detachment coupled with precise observation, attention and perfect timing and reaction. Unless a state of absolute sympathy exists between the pot, the kiln and the Rakuist that indispensable balance between the forces and their state of flux will not be achieved.

Although Raku firing has to be the product of personal sensibilities and control, it is a great advantage to have the services of an assistant during glaze firing. It is, of course, imperative that he understands the process and is able to work with you in complete accord. It is extremely helpful to be able to hand over to the assistant the routine matters of stoking and damping the kiln as well as having his assistance for the removal and replacement of the saggar lid while you are concerned with handling the pot itself.

11 Secondary reduction and quenching

It is not always possible to follow the ideal precedents of Japanese kiln designs because of difficulties in obtaining suitable fuels – this has led to the evolution of new designs that fire efficiently on fuels more widely available. Unfortunately these Raku wares lack some of the characteristics of the originals and therefore post-glazing modifications to the process have been incorporated.

In Japan the red Raku is removed from the red-hot kiln and allowed to air-cool, while the black wares are quickly taken from the strong reducing atmosphere of the kiln chamber and subjected to the sudden ordeal of being quenched in cold water. This quenching causes the glaze to change from a fluid to a solid state almost instantaneously, thereby 'freezing in' the colour and surface effects brought about by the strong reduction process.

Most Raku in the West attempts to follow the pattern of the 'black' firing technique but generally the kilns and fuels employed give rise to a much weaker degree of reduction in the kiln chamber than their Japanese counterparts. In order to avoid the rather 'thin' and garish appearances that tend to result, a final heavy reduction substitute has been developed for Western style Raku. This involves an intermediate reduction stage between the removal of the form from the kiln and its quenching in water.

This modification of technique probably owes its genesis, in some measure at least, to the misinterpretation and misplacement of the 'carbon shadow' process in the traditional sequence, to which it is very similar. Also, the effects obtained by the Western secondary reduction technique are remarkably dramatic and surprising, creating sudden changes of colour and surface texture as well as areas of strong lustre, all of which effects are very much in keeping with Occidental ideas of what creates visual excitement, but which would be thought to be much too unsubtle and ostentatious by those educated in the tradition of Teaism.

Clear burning may be basically interpreted as combustion in the presence of a sufficiently ample supply of available oxygen, both to combine with any free carbon in the kiln atmosphere and also to maintain the existence of oxides within the glaze mix in their oxide form. If the supply of oxygen is reduced the resulting imbalance between oxygen and carbon produces a kiln atmosphere in which hot carbon exists in a free and uncombined state (smoke). Also, the need for oxygen in the atmosphere is so great that metallic oxides, for example, are robbed of that element and are thereby reduced to their base metals and display the appropriate colour characteristics. (For example, oxidized copper is green in colour while reduced copper is the colour of copper metal.) This kiln condition of oxygen starvation is normally referred to simply as 'reduction', but in the Raku context it is more clearly described as 'primary reduction'.

One must remember that Raku wares are withdrawn from the kiln while the glaze is still in a liquid state and as long as this state is maintained the glaze will undergo chemical changes in response to the prevailing atmospheric conditions and will also react with a variety of chemical substances (such as bismuth or certain metallic salts) if they are applied directly to the glaze surface.

Raku glaze remains fluid for only a minute or two after the pot has been removed from the kiln. This is but a very brief period in which to achieve a substantial reduction effect and it is therefore important that the densest reducing atmosphere is achieved as rapidly as possible. This has been found to be most easily obtainable through taking the red-hot pot directly from the kiln and enclosing it in a lidded metal container filled with readily combustible matter such as sawdust, dry leaves or woodshavings. The heat from the pot instantly causes combustion to take place, consuming oxygen, creating a source of hot free carbon and developing a strong reducing atmosphere in the immediate vicinity of the pot.

Since the glaze is still very soft it is also given textural effects from the direct contact with the combustible materials in which it lies and often absorbs fragments of the burning matter directly into herself.

Parts of the form that were left bare during glaze application readily take up the free carbon in the secondary reduction atmosphere and become transformed in colour to a smoky grey or, if left in the reduction chamber for a longer period of time, a dense matt black.

The combustion of leaves or sawdust that takes place within the secondary reduction chamber produces a considerable degree of heat in its own right, which decreases the rate of heat loss from the Raku pot. This results in an extension of the time during which the glaze remains in a fluid form and is receptive to the effects of the prevailing reducing atmosphere.

The effects of the reduction diminish rapidly when the piece is removed from the secondary reduction chamber.

The duration of the secondary reduction stage in the Raku process has to be gauged by personal experience and will depend upon the degree of reduction that is required. Normally a period of reduction of between two and five minutes will achieve effects ranging from slight to extreme.

In order to retain these effects the pot must be quenched in cold water immediately it is removed from the combustion chamber. Any delay causes a rapid diminution of the typical reduction qualities, as re-oxidation takes place as soon as an ample supply of oxygen is again available.

Occasionally random surface effects other than those obtainable through secondary reduction are desired. These may be achieved by the addition of various chemicals directly on to the surface of the glaze immediately following the removal of the pot from the kiln and before it is placed in the combustion chamber. The materials most commonly used are grog and the salts of copper, silver, bismuth and tin. These may be applied by dipping, splashing, dripping or spraying. It is vital that whatever method of application is employed it be effected with considerable speed since any delay allows the glaze to cool and therefore reduces the time during which it is receptive to chemical change.

The degree of reduction that is achieved in the combustion chamber is dependent on two factors other than the length of the reduction period. The first concerns the heat of the Raku piece when it is initially introduced into the chamber and how rapidly it cools once it is there. A high initial temperature is effected by an efficient and practised routine worked out between the Rakuist and his assistant so that the transfer from saggar to combustible materials is not delayed. Thin forms cool more rapidly than thick ones and consequently they will neither maintain combustion nor a glaze capable of being affected by the reducing atmosphere as long as the thicker pieces. The second factor affecting reduction is the nature of the combustible matter used to obtain the reduction. A material with a small particle size that is soft and easy burning and dry rather than damp is most suitable. Dry leaves, grass, straw, sawdust, fine wood-shavings and processed paper industrial packing are all excellent for Raku and each have slightly different effects.

If the piece is completely buried in the combustible matter a strong reduction will take place over the whole form. It is usually advantageous to throw a handful of sawdust into the inside of a form if reduction is particularly desired there.

On occasion reduction is required on a certain part of the form, in which case it is preferable to use the combustion chamber uncovered and to place the piece in sawdust in such a way that only the part to be reduced has direct contact with it. Those parts of the form not in direct contact with the burning matter will retain a primarily oxidized appearance. Alternatively, the whole piece may be reduced but, when quenched, only the part to retain reduced characteristics should be immersed – the rest of the form may be allowed to partly re-oxidize through contact with the air.

Areas of slight lustre re-oxidize very easily and rapidly. If lustres are definitely desired a long period of dense reduction is advisable, followed by a very rapid transfer to cold water. Alternatively, pieces may be left to cool by themselves, completely buried in sawdust.

If a more traditional effect is desired (particularly important for the *kuro* substitute glazes) a dense final reduction has to be achieved without impairing the glaze surface with marks from direct contact with the reducing agent or with the ostentatious spots of lustre, which come from close proximity to the same burning matter.

An alternative secondary reduction chamber may be constructed which will satisfy these requirements (fig. 40), consisting of a lidded metal drum containing a substitute saggar made from expanded metal. The spaces between the walls of the drum are packed with a smoke producing material (a mixture of dry leaves and hair produces a particularly dense and suitable smoke for this purpose). The drum is heated gently from the outside with the flame gun while the pot is being fired (or a small fire may be lit beneath the drum as shown) so that the pot is retained in a state receptive to the effects of reduction for as long as possible when it is transferred to the reduction chamber from the kiln. Immediately before removing the pot from the kiln the combustibles in the chamber are ignited (again with the flame gun or some substitute). The pot is then removed from the kiln and placed in the expanded metal chamber and the drum covered with the lid, thereby producing a very effective substitute for strong primary reduction.

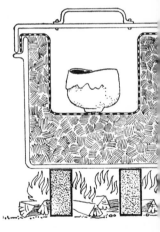

Fig. 40
Alternative type of secondary reduction chamber

Quenching and soaking

The main purpose of quenching the pot in water immediately after it is removed from the secondary reduction chamber is to 'freeze' the effects of reduction. Any delay between these two stages causes the effects of reduction to become diminished through re-oxidation.

The maximum 'freezing' effects are obtained through quenching in cold water Some very thin forms, however, as well as those that have been made by joining a number of sections and some of the special throwing Raku bodies tend to suffer damage at this stage of the process. The dangers can be reduced by quenching the pots in hot water rather than cold. Raku bottles and cylinder forms should always be quenched by being eased down into the water in a mouth-upwards position so that the water can run slowly into the interior. If these forms are quenched in an inverted position shattering often results.

Quenching causes the Raku glaze to craze, opening up minute fissures in the glaze film down to the porous body beneath. In order to accentuate the decorative effect of the crazing some Raku potters quench and soak their pots in strong tea which leaves a deposit within the glaze fissures and forms a decorative device. Generally Chajin consider this to be an undesirable affectation and much inferior to a similar effect resulting from actual use. However, as a means of decoration it can be very effectively employed and stronger effects than are obtainable from tea may be achieved through soaking the pot overnight in various dyestuffs or stains.

After quenching the pots should be scrubbed with a stiff brush and water and allowed to dry. Often surface effects, particularly lustres, are hidden beneath an obscuring film which may be removed by scrubbing with mud or some mild abrasive before washing and drying.

Conclusion

Sen-no-Rikyu, Chajin of unequalled refinement, artistic genius, innovator, Man-of-Zen, founder-patron of Raku and major contributor to Japanese aesthetic development, died by his own hand in the year 1591.

Rikyu's ceremony of *seppuku* (honourable suicide by cutting the stomach) was performed at the Daitokuji Temple, headquarters of the Rinzai, or sudden enlightenment, sect of Zen, the temple with which he had been associated for many years. His death was ordered by his former patron, the awesome military dictator of all Japan, Toyotomi Hideyoshi, for a minor, if indeed any, offence.

However unfair were the circumstances of his death it was perhaps to his greater glory that this famous aesthete died through a self-inflicted act of extreme personal ordeal of the kind that could be contemplated only by one in possession of supreme self-discipline.

The unique talents of Rikyu, in association with the sculptural refinement of Chojiro, had been responsible for establishing the Raku art as a process of beautification through ordeal and self-discipline that has stood for fourteen generations as a microcosm of the Zen-based *wabi* spirit.

Appendices

Assessing kiln temperature from visible colour

°C	Colour	
Below 475	Black	
475	First visible redness	
650	Dark red	
775	Cherry red	
815	Bright cherry red	⎫ Western-
900	Orange-red	⎬ style Raku
950–1000	Orange (traditional red Raku)	⎭
1090	Yellow	
1200	Pale yellow (black Raku)	

Note on lead poisoning

Lead and other heavy metals such as cadmium, barium, selenium, zinc and antimony are all toxic and present health hazards should they be absorbed into the body. In the case of Raku the dangers of plumbism are particularly prevalent and considerable precaution in the use of lead chemicals is recommended.

The use of pure forms of lead oxide are especially dangerous and great care should be exercised to ensure that airborne particles of this substance are not breathed into the lungs.

Glazes containing lead are susceptible to attack from acids (particularly when they are underfired or in combination with boron, both of which commonly occur in Raku). Raku pots glazed with lead based glazes should not be used as food containers or regularly as drinking wares. Lead glazes are particularly prone to attack from the following foodstuffs:

> Fruit juices (citric acid)
> Apple juice (malic acid)
> Coffee (succinic acid)
> Vinegar (acetic acid)

Lead may be introduced into Raku glazes in the comparatively safe form of a low solubility frit, thus eliminating the primary dangers of using the element.

Suppliers of ceramic materials

Australia

Ceramic Art Supplies, 53 Pulteney Street, Adelaide 5000
Ceramic Supply Co., 61 Lakemba Street, Belmore, New South Wales 2192
Harrison & Crosfield (ANZ) Ltd, 17–27 Newstead Avenue, Newstead, Brisbane, Queensland
Harrison & Crosfield (ANZ) Ltd., 331 Murray Street, Perth, Western Australia
Newbold General Refractories, Toogood Avenue, Beverley, South Australia
Potters' Workshop, 28 Greenaway Street, Bulleen, Victoria 3105
Rodda & Co., (SA) Pty Ltd., Eastern Parade, Rosewater, South Australia
Russell Cowan Pty Ltd., 136 Pacific Highway, Waitara, N.S.W. 2077

South Australian Studio, Potters' Club Inc., 16 Sussex Street, North Adelaide 5006
Walker Ceramics, Boronia Road, Watsonia, Victoria 3087

For additional information contact:
The Potters' Society of Australia, 97a Bourke Street, Woolloomooloo, N.S.W. 2011

Canada

Clayburn Harbison Ltd, 1690 West Broadway, Vancouver, British Columbia
Greater Toronto Ceramic Centre, 167 Lakeshore Road, Toronto 14, Ontario
A. P. Green Firebrick Co., Rosemount Avenue, Weston, Ontario
Mercedes Ceramic Supply, 8 Wallace Street, Woodbridge, Ontario
Pottery Supply House, 491 Wildwood Road, Oakville, Ontario

England

British Ceramic Service Co. Ltd, Bricesco House, 1 Park Avenue, Wolstanton, Newcastle, Staffs
Fulham Pottery, 210 New Kings Road, London SW6
Pike Brothers, Wareham, Dorset
W. Podmore & Sons Ltd, Caledonian Mills, Shelton, Stoke-on-Trent, Staffs
Alex Tiranti Ltd, 73 Charlotte Street, London W1
Wengers Ltd, Etruria, Stoke-on-Trent, Staffs

New Zealand

Clive Pottery Studio, 203 Parnell Road, Auckland 1
A. C. Emery, 14 Kohimarama Road, Auckland 5
Allan Hedger, 94 Federal Street, Auckland 1
Riverside Potteries, R.D. 2 Amberley, Christchurch
Titian Pottery Ltd, Great South Road, Takanini

USA

Cedar Heights Clay Co., Oak Hill, Ohio 45656
Ceramic Color and Chemical Manufacturing Co., Block House Run Road, New Brighton, Pennsylvania 15066
DFC Ceramics, 2401 East 40th Avenue, Denver, Colorado 80205
Ferro Corporation, 4150 East 56th Street, Cleveland, Ohio 44105
General Refractories Co., 7640 West Chicago Avenue, Detroit, Michigan 48204
Hammill & Gillespie Inc., 255 Broadway, New York, N.Y. 10007
O. Hommel Co., Hope Street, Carnegie, Pennsylvania 15106
Pemco-Glidden-Durkee Division of SCM Corporation, 5601 Eastern Avenue, Baltimore, Maryland 21224
Standard Ceramics, 9 Sansbury Street, Carnegie, Pennsylvania 15106
Western Ceramic Supply Co., 1601 Howard Street, San Francisco, California 94103
Jack D. Wolfe Co. Inc., 724 Meeker Avenue, Brooklyn, New York, N.Y. 11222

Bibliography

Dickerson, J. *Fourteen Generations of Raku Ceramics*. Anglo–Japanese Financial Institute

Dodd, A. E. *Dictionary of Ceramics*. London: Newnes; New Jersey: Littlefield Adams 1967

Fukukita, Y. *Cha-no-yu*. Tokyo: Maruzen Co. 1932.

Hayashiya, S. 'Koetsu Chawan', *Tosetsu 61*. Nihon Toji Kyokai

Hisamatsu, S. *Zen and the Fine Arts*. California: Kodansha International 1971

Isono, F. *Toki Zenshu 6 – Chojiro and Koetsu*. Tokyo: Heibonsha 1958

Jenyns, S. *Japanese Pottery*. London: Faber & Faber 1971

Koyama, F. 'Momoyama', *Sekai Toji Zenshu*, vol. 3. Tokyo: Zauho Press 1955

Leach, B. *A Potter's Book*. London: Faber & Faber; New York: Transatlantic Arts 1945

Leach, B. *Kenzan and his Tradition: the Life and Times of Koyetsu, Sotatsu, Korin and Kenzan*. London: Faber & Faber 1966

Lee, S. *Tea Taste in Japanese Art*. The Asia Society of New York 1963

Lynggard, F. *Raku*. Copenhagen: Clausens Forlag 1970

Miller, R. A. *Japanese Ceramics*. Toto Shupan Co., Tuttle

Mitsoaka, T. *Ceramic Art of Japan*. Tokyo: Japan Tourist Library 1953

Munsterberg, H. *Zen and Oriental Art*. Tuttle
The Ceramic Art of Japan – a Handbook for Collectors, Tuttle 1964

Nitobe, I. *Japanese Traits and Foreign Influence*. London: Kegan Paul 1927

Oda, E. 'Nonko', *Tosetu 61*. Nihon Toji Kyokai

Okakura, K. *The Book of Tea*. New York: Dover

Raku Kichizaemon 'Chojiro and Nonko', *Sekai Toji Zenshu*, vol. 7. Tokyo: Zauho Press 1955

Rhodes, D. *Clays and Glazes for the Potter*. Philadelphia: Chilton 1957; London: Pitman 1958
Kilns: Design, Construction and Operation. London: Pitman; Philadelphia: Chilton 1970

Sanders, H. H. *The World of Japanese Ceramics*. California: Kodansha International 1967

Sadler, A. L. *Cha-no-yu, the Japanese Tea Ceremony*. Tuttle 1960

Suzuki, D. T. *Zen and Japanese Culture*. London: Routledge; New York: Pantheon 1959
Essays in Zen Buddhism. London: Rider & Co.; New York: Grove Press 1953

Tsunoda, R. *Sources of Japanese Tradition*. New York: Columbia University Press 1964

Glossary

AKA RAKU   Red style Raku. Dates from first generation of Raku.

AMAYA (Sasaki Sokei)   Korean potter. Emigrated to Japan. Father of Chojiro.

ARAMOMI   Press method of wedging clay.

ASHIKAGA PERIOD   Kyoto shogunate (1338–1568). Politically weak but culturally progressive period.

BALL CLAY   Fine grained, white firing clay used to impart plasticity to a clay body.

BAT (Drying)   A slab of plaster of Paris used to dry soft clay.

BENTONITE   Very fine grained clay type. An effective plasticizer.

BISQUE WARE   Unglazed ceramic ware which has had a low preliminary firing and has thereby been freed of chemically combined water.

CALCINE   To heat a substance until it loses chemically combined water and volatile gases.

CARBON SHADOW DECORATION   Decorative carbon stains deposited on red Raku bisque wares and later trapped under semi-transparent glaze.

CHA-DAMARI   'Tea pool' depression at the base of *chawan* to collect the last drops of tea.

CHA-E   The early name given to Tea gatherings.

CHAJIN   Man-of-Tea, Tea Master.

CH'AN BUDDHISM   Chinese school of Buddhism. The Chinese version of Zen.

CHA-NO-YU   Japanese Tea Ceremony. Known as *Cha-no-yu* after the time of Jo-wo and Rikyu.

CHASEN   Hand-made bamboo whisk for mixing powder tea.

CHASEN-ZURI   The part of a *chawan* in which the tea is whisked.

CHAWAN   Tea bowl.

CHOJIRO   First Raku Master. Received the title posthumously from Hideyoshi.

CHONYU   Raku Master of the seventh generation.

CLAY BODY   A calculated composition of various clays, designed to satisfy specific requirements.

CRAZE   Cracking of the glaze film.

DAIMYO   Literally 'great name', i.e. feudal lord.

DAITOKU-JI   Famous temple in northern Kyoto at which Rikyu studied. It is the headquarters of the Rinzai sect of Zen.

DAMPER   A device that closes the chimney of a kiln. In Raku kilns dampers are also used to control air supply to the kiln.

DOGEN   1200–53. Founder of Soto sect of Zen in Japan.

DONYU   See NONKO.

DORAKU   Younger brother of Nonko. Maker of *Waki-gama* Raku.

DUNT   Cracking or shattering of wares on cooling.

EARTHENWARE CLAY   Low firing clay, usually red in colour due to iron content.

EISAI   1141–1215. Founder of the Lin-chi (Rinzai) sect of Zen in Japan.

FIREBRICK   A fireclay refractory brick capable of withstanding high temperatures. Used for building the walls of Raku kilns.

FIRECLAY   A refractory clay. The plastic varieties make an excellent basis for a Raku clay body.

FLUX   A material which promotes fusion and melt in glazes.

FRIT   The melting together of a group of ceramic materials to form a compound which is then cooled and re-ground to a powder form. Frits are made for the purpose of eliminating such undesirable properties as solubility or toxicity.

FUDE   The versatile pointed Japanese brush used for calligraphy and decoration.

FUNORI   Japanese glaze gum, made from boiled seaweed.

FUSE   To melt together.

GAKU   Hill, peak or mountain. Refers to the 'hills' which form the rim of Raku chawan. Five is the most common number of hills (known as *gogaku*).

GANPAKU   See SOTAN.

GLAZE   A glassy substance which is fused on to the surfaces of ceramic wares.

GREEN WARE   Wares which are dry but have not yet received a bisque firing.

GROG   Reground, hard fired clay added to Raku clay bodies to promote resistance to thermal shock.

HAKE   Flat Japanese brush used for applying wide areas of pigment, slip or glaze.

HAKEME BRUSH   Home-made brush of rice straw or grass, much used in Korea and Japan for applying vigorous slip decoration.

HARA-KIRI.   See SEPPUKU.

HIDEYOSHI   See TOYOTOMI.

HON-GAMA   'Main kiln' – the wares produced only by the official Raku Masters.

ICHINYU   Raku Master of the fourth generation.

ICHIGEN   Son of Ichinyu. Maker of *Waki-gama* Raku.

IDO WARE   Korean peasant wares favoured by Chajin for their simplicity and faithfulness to the spirit of *wabi*.

INLAY   See MISHIMA.

JOKEI (Kichizemon Jokei)   Received the Raku seal from Hideyoshi in memory of the achievements of Chojiro. Also received the title 'Best in the World'. Raku Master of the second generation.

JO-WO   Chajin. Teacher of Tea to Rikyu.

KAMOGAWA-ISHI   A stone dredged from Kyoto's Kamo river and used as the basis of *kamoguro*. The stone is rich in both iron and manganese.

KAMOGURO   Black Raku glaze, also known as *kuro* Raku.

KAOLIN   Pure primary clay.

KESHIKI   Term in the Japanese aesthetics of ceramics referring to the desirability of variation, softness and a slightly damp appearance.

KEINYU   Raku Master of the eleventh generation.

KENZAN (Ogata Kenzan)   Famous potter of the Tokugawa period. Studied under Ninsei and Ichinyu.

KICHIZAEMON   Raku Master of the fourteenth generation.

KILN   A furnace for firing ceramic wares.

KOETSU (Hon'ami Koetsu)   One of Japan's most famous artists with great ability in many arts. Studied Raku under Jokei and Nonko.

KOGO   Incense box.

KOICHA   Thick tea – the first tea course in *Cha-no-yu*.

KONYU   Raku Master of the twelfth generation.

KUCHU (Hon'ami Koho)   Grandson of Koetsu. Made Raku, influenced by his grandfather and Shigaraki wares.

KURO RAKU   Black Raku glaze, also known as *kamoguro*.

KUSHI   Wooden rib with teeth for combing patterns in clay and slip.

LEAD   The basic glaze flux in Raku.

LUTE   Method of joining slabs of leather-hard clay by means of clay slip.

MAKU GUSURI   A Raku glaze style developed by Nonko, in which welts of glaze run down the form in a controlled way to create an effect reminiscent of draped fabric.

MATURITY   The point at which clay hardens to its maximum strength and the point at which glaze achieves complete fusion.

MISHIMA   A decoration of contrasting coloured clay inlayed into a clay form.

MOMOYAMA PERIOD   1568–1615. The period between Nobunaga's seizure of power in Kyoto and the establishment of the régime of the Tokugawas.

NAGARE   Raku glaze style developed by Nonko, reminiscent of tear-drops on the underside of bowl forms.

NEJIMOMI   Screw method of wedging clay.

NINSEI   Famous potter. Specialist in overglaze enamel decoration.

NOBUNAGA   See ODA NOBUNAGA.

NONKO   (Donyu). Raku Master of the third generation. Major innovator and one of Japan's greatest Masters of the *chawan* form.

ODA NOBUNAGA   Daimyo and warlord who, with the assistance of Hideyoshi, ended the Ashikaga shogunate and established the Momoyama era.

OMOTE SENGE RYU   Famous school of *Cha-no-yu* in Kyoto run by the direct descendants of Rikyu.

OXIDES OF METALS   Materials most commonly used to impart colour to glazes.

OXIDIZING FIRE   A kiln atmosphere in possession of an ample supply of oxygen.

PADDLE Flat wooden form used in place of a blunger to mix clay slip or a small wooden tool used to shape pots.

PCE Pyrometric cone equivalent.

PLASTICITY The quality which allows a clay to be freely shaped and manipulated and to retain that form as it dries without cracking.

PLASTIC VITROX Californian earth mineral with similarities to potash feldspar.

PYROMETER Instrument used for measuring kiln temperatures.

QUENCH To cool red-hot Raku quickly by plunging it into water.

RAKU Chinese character meaning 'ease', 'pleasure' or 'enjoyment'.

RAKU YAKI The ceramic wares made by the Raku family of Kyoto for use in *Cha-no-yu*.

RECONSTITUTION OF CLAY Treating dry but unfired clay with water in order to return it to a plastic state.

REDUCTION FIRING A kiln atmosphere deficient in oxygen.

REFRACTORY Capable of withstanding very high temperatures.

RIB A bamboo tool used to assist in throwing. Normally used in Raku for throwing saggars.

RIKYU (Sen-no-Rikyu). Aesthete of the Momoyama period. The most famous of all Chajin, he reconceived the *Cha-no-yu* along accentuated Zen lines. Raku patron and collaborator with Chojiro in the conception and perfection of Raku *chawan* forms.

ROJI The path and garden that accompanies a Tea house.

RYONYU Raku Master of the ninth generation.

SABI Term in the aesthetics of *Cha-no-yu* meaning 'to be mellowed and beautified by use'.

SAGGAR A cylindrical fireclay box which forms the firing chamber of Raku kilns.

SAKAZUKI Drinking cup for rice wine.

SANYU Raku Master of the sixth generation.

SATORI The state of consciousness of the Buddha-mind. Zen enlightenment.

SEINYU Raku Master of the thirteenth generation.

SEPPUKU Honourable suicide by cutting the stomach. The characters may also be read as *hara-kiri*.

SGRAFFITO Incised decoration scratched into the clay surface.

SHIRATAMA A Japanese lead boro-silicate frit.

SHIRO RAKU White style Raku glazing developed by Jokei (Raku II).

SHOGUN Military dictator. Officially '*generalissimo*' to the Emperor.

SHUKO (Murata Shuko) Tea aesthete of the Ashikaga period.

SICCATIVE A gum or agent used to secure a stable film of under- or over-glaze enamels, colours or glazes.

SINTER The beginning of cohesion within the glaze film, effected by increasing temperature.

SLIP Clay or glaze particles suspended in water.

SONYU Raku Master of the fifth generation.

SOTAN (Sen Sotan or Ganpaku). Grandson of Rikyu. A famous Chajin and patron of Raku.

SPODUMENE A natural lithium alumino-silicate.

SUKIYA House of *Cha-no-yu* gatherings.

SUNG DYNASTY Chinese dynasty, 960–1279, under which Ch'an Buddhism prospered and powder-tea drinking was introduced.

TANAKA SOKEI Raku potter of the first generation. Collaborated with Chojiro and Rikyu. Father of Jokei.

TATAMI Japanese floor matting.

TEA The philosophy and aesthetic of *Cha-no-yu*.

TEMMOKU 'Rabbit fur' glaze of the Sung dynasty – influenced Ch'an taste. *Temmoku* is also understood as a shape in Japan and influenced the work of Chojiro and Jokei.

TEDORI Term in the Japanese aesthetics of ceramics, concerning the relationship between 'visual weight' and actual weight.

TEIRIN Potter. Mother of Chojiro. Wife of Amaya. After her husband's death she made wares known as *Ama yaki* (Nun's ware).

THERMAL SHOCK Severe stresses caused in a ceramic form by sudden temperature changes.

TOKUGAWA IEYASU   *Daimyo* and statesman whose dynasty succeeded the fall of the House of Toyotomi.

TOKUNYU   Raku Master of the eighth generation.

TONG MARK   The mark left in the soft Raku glaze by the tongs used to remove the piece from the kiln.

TOYOTOMI HIDEYOSHI   Pacifier and Dictator of Japan after the death of Nobunaga. Patron of Rikyu and the Raku.

URA SENGE RYU   Famous school of *Cha-no-yu* in Kyoto run by the direct descendants of Rikyu.

USUCHA   Thin tea, the second tea course in *Cha-no-yu.*

VIEWING TUBE   Tube which allows the Rakuist to see directly into the saggar during glaze firing.

VITRIFY   To become dense and 'glassy' through the application of heat.

WABI   The basis of Rikyu's *Cha-no-yu.* The aesthetics of simplicity, asymmetry and unpretentious naturalness.

WAKI GAMA   'Colateral kiln' – all Raku not made by the official Masters.

WAX RESIST   Decorative use of painted wax to resist oxide, slip or glaze.

YAKI   Ceramic ware.

YOSHIMASSA (Ashikaga Yoshimassa)   Shogun. Patron of Zen and *Cha-e.*

ZANGURISHITA   Term in the Japanese aesthetics of ceramics concerned with agreeable texture. A slight roughness is most desirable.

ZEN BUDDHISM   A non-theistic religion devoted to the achievement of Buddha nature through personal effort.